AI & The Data Revolution

How Teams can Harness Disruption to Conquer Turmoil

Laura B. Madsen

DATA—
DRIVEN
AI

www.technicspub.com/ai

Technics Publications
SEDONA, ARIZONA

115 Linda Vista
Sedona, AZ 86336 USA
https://www.TechnicsPub.com

Edited by Sadie Hoberman

Cover design by Lorena Molinari

First Printing 2024

Copyright © 2024 by Laura B. Madsen

ISBN, print ed.	9781634624480
ISBN, Kindle ed.	9781634624497
ISBN, PDF ed.	9781634624602

To my Uncle William, thanks for showing me the way.

Acknowledgments

It takes a village. In the case of this book, it's a big village. The research for a book like this is such an important part of the process. I read anything I could get my hands on. I watched countless videos and spoke to many experts. The trouble with discussing these huge topics with experts when you are not an expert is that you may not know the right questions to ask. Or, as I learned plenty of times in this process, what you thought you knew is a tiny fragment of what is available to know. In addition, the fast pace of change helped to complicate matters. Just as I was finishing this work, there were no fewer than twenty-five AI frameworks from governing bodies and countries. The AI experts I interviewed did their very best to educate me. *Any mistakes, misinterpretations, or misunderstandings are completely mine.* Tom Niccum, Juan Sequeda, Melanie Mitchell, PhD, Kirsten Hoogenakker, Taisa Kushner, PhD, Steve Case, and the team at Semantic Arts, among others who had "off-the-record" conversations with me.

Many thanks go to:

Tom Niccum, who bore the brunt of ill-informed questions and was ever so patient as I finally "figured it out." Without his knowledge and support, this book would not be in your hands.

Juan Sequeda, from texts to emails and a couple of conversations over cocktails, Juan's passion for the topic helped inspire my interest.

Serena Roberts, who accidentally inspired this book by just trying to make Moxy a grown-up company that efficiently uses resources. Very few people push me past my comfort zone like she does. I'm grateful.

It's a little surreal to thank the "Moxy Team" because when you dream something and then it happens, sometimes it still feels like a dream. It is an absolute dream to work with Anna Lindquist, Ken Flerlage, Kevin Flerlage, and Ruby Hoffman. Each read early copies, dissuaded me from using words like "interwebs," and helped shape this from a rough draft to a well-honed deliverable.

Steve Case, who answered my (borderline panicked) request to help inform me on the finer points of knowledge graphs. Steve and the team, including the venerable Dave McComb, have been at this for a while. It shows.

A big thank you to Steve Hoberman and the team at Technics. This is my fourth industry book. My first books were published by a big house, and I had very little interaction with anyone there. Life is different when you're an author with Technics. They know you; you know them. You get to meet other authors and support each other as you create. Steve reads every word. There is no comparison.

A big thanks to a large cadre of family and friends, including my son Nolan, my siblings, and Dad. As life marched on and my deadline loomed, family obligations often took a back seat. Thanks for understanding. Finally, I want to thank my husband, Karl Madsen (always my first reader), for his incredible patience, support, and love. I would not be the person I am today without him.

Contents

Prologue _____ 1

Chapter 1: What this is, What it is not _____ 5

Chapter 2: Let's Get it Started! _____ 11
A Brief History Lesson _____ 12
Data, Data Everywhere _____ 16
Once Upon a Time in a Place Called Silicon Valley _____ 18
Not All Data is Equal _____ 23
Speed and Scale _____ 26
Let's Not do Dumb Stuff Faster _____ 27
Kwality is Job One _____ 29
Would you like AI with that? _____ 33
But, like, how?! _____ 35

Chapter 3: Getting Future-Ready _____ 39
Knowledge Graphs _____ 43
Point-Solutions _____ 46
Hybrid Theory _____ 47

Chapter 4: Disruption in Modern Times _____ 51
Something from Nothing _____ 58
What is a Thought Model? _____ 59
Sustainable Disruption Model _____ 60
Disrupters | Optimizers | Keepers Profiles _____ 63
    Disrupters _____ 63
    Optimizers _____ 67
    Keepers _____ 70
How to use SDM _____ 73
A Moment for Keepers _____ 75

Chapter 5: All that Glitters _____ 77
Generations Speak _____ 78
Technology and Pace of Change _____ 82
It's Not Just About Leadership _____ 89

The Myths of Disruption _____ 91
   Myth Number One _____ 91
   Myth Number Two _____ 92
   Myth Number Three _____ 93
   Myth Number Four _____ 94
   Myth Number Five _____ 95
Teams and Maturity _____ 97
But, like how? _____ 98

Chapter 6: Are You Ready for it? _____ 101
Building a Mystery _____ 102
Culture Club _____ 103
But, First, the Elephant _____ 105
Disrupting Data Teams _____ 109
The Re-org _____ 111
Achilles Heel _____ 112

Chapter 7: SDM and a Framework for AI __ 115
Who: Find Your People _____ 117
Why: State Your Intention _____ 118
What: Deciding what to Build _____ 119
How: Methods to Collaborate, Cultivate, Create, and Communicate 120
When: Setting Expectations _____ 120
How Much: Metrics to Prove Value _____ 121
Variations on a Theme _____ 122
   People Power (Who Section) _____ 122
   Identify Use Cases (How Section) _____ 122
   Testing Methodologies (What Section) _____ 123

Chapter 8: Governance with a Capital G___ 131
Governance Definitions _____ 134
   Access Governance _____ 134
   Corporate Governance _____ 134
   Data Governance _____ 135
   Information Governance _____ 135
   Portfolio Governance _____ 136
Governing is a Four-Letter Word _____ 137
   Increasing Data Usage _____ 139
   Improving Data Quality _____ 139
   Identifying Data Lineage _____ 139
   Ensuring Data Protection _____ 140

Top Four AI Governance Considerations _____ 141
   Top-Down_____ 142
   Policies _____ 142
   K.I.S.S. (keep it simple, silly) _____ 142
   Flexibility is Strength_____ 143
Time Keeps on Ticking (ticking, ticking) into the Future _____ 144
Governance Structure _____ 145
Do the Right Thing _____ 146
   A Little Less Conversation, a Little More Action, Please_____ 149
   Know When to Hold 'em (Accountable)_____ 152
The Reckoning_____ 154

Chapter 9: Welcome to the Real World ____155
I Wanna Push You Around _____ 156
It's Not Me It's You _____ 157
Mad Skills _____ 161
I Do Not Think it Means What You Think it Means _____ 163
Psychic Friends Network_____ 165
When you're a Hammer _____ 166
Winter is Coming _____ 166
Bitter with the Sweet _____ 168

Chapter 10: Step by Step _____169
What's your Type? _____ 171
From the Top _____ 172
Missing You_____ 173
Tech Debt Deprecation Plan _____ 175
Moving On, Letting Go _____ 178
Oversight and Operations _____ 179
A Better Future _____ 180
How to Deploy the Framework_____ 182
Create, Cultivate, Collaborate, Communicate _____ 182
Examples _____ 184
   Starting from Zero Got Nothing to Lose_____ 185
   A Different Outcome_____ 187
   It's Complicated _____ 189
   A Different Outcome_____ 190
Fade to Black _____ 191

Appendix _____ 193
Book List _____ 193
Table of Contents for AI Framework Playbook _____ 195
Technical Debt Brief _____ 196

Index _____ 197

Prologue

The most meaningful things in my life have come from a culmination of events and experiences. I suppose that's true for everyone. But as I started the process of writing and researching this book, several things had come to roost. Of course, there are the basic things like getting a book proposal accepted. Then having the wherewithal to write the thing. But there are also bigger things. Long planted seeds of critical thinking and contrarian views. Pessimism and an overwhelming rebellious attitude that has only increased with age. The pivotal action, the one that pushed me off the ledge, was a peek into 2024.

In the fall of 2023, my business partner, Serena Roberts, and I, took a little get-away to plan for the upcoming year. We dedicate time to think about what we want for the next year. We include some fun activities, and a little brown liquor (for me, anyway) helps to clear the cobwebs. Serena had planned the trip to Stillwater, Minnesota. A pretty river town with cute shops, cool boutique hotels, and a lot of non-chain restaurants. The first day went amazeballs. We followed the standard agile retro. We asked ourselves what went well, what didn't go well, and what we would change.

The next day, the big item on the agenda was what to do about me. I tend to be the "problem child." I'm restless. I get bored at the drop of a hat. Sometimes, I am so contrarian that it seems nothing will please me (my therapist says I'm very self-aware). That morning, I was in full form. Serena mentioned the use of ChatGPT for some of our marketing efforts. As a small services firm, anything we can do to improve our marketing efficiency is important. So, when she mentioned it, I'm sure she thought, "Of course we will use this. Laura's a reasonable person. Nothing to worry about." What she got was a 15-minute diatribe about the dangers lurking in AI, how the only thing that I provided as value to our company (maybe the world) could now be deduced to prompt engineering. As Serena often does, she let me rant for a while. Then she attempted to rationalize with me, and when that didn't work, she gave me the space to work through it. Ten days later, we reconvened. What occurred in those ten days is the culmination of a lifetime of work.

I do mean a lifetime. From a very young age, I wanted to be an entrepreneur. I started several "businesses" before I was 10. I sold door-to-door so often, my neighbors saw me coming and got out their checkbooks. When I wasn't doing that, you could find me with my back against a tree reading. I loved STEM and took every opportunity to learn more, despite a lack of support from most of my teachers. I would go on to get a Master of Science degree in Applied Psychology. I used to describe it as an applied analytics degree. I was taught statistical methods to control errors in data. It was after school that I started, unbeknownst to me, my career in data and analytics.

Even in my early career, I was not a trend follower. In 2006, when an executive asked me about building a dashboard, I told him it was a trend. "Don't waste the money on the software." (I never claimed to be a futurist.) I wrote some books on data in healthcare. Then, a book on data governance. I generally kept pace with what was happening in the industry, from "big data" to machine learning (ML) and artificial intelligence (AI). Keeping pace, though, meant my pessimistic side was staying vigilant, and I didn't like what I was seeing. When ChatGPT was released to the public, everyone went bananas. Within a few days, I saw books on Amazon that had been "written in three days" by ChatGPT. It felt like the proverbial rug had been pulled out from under me when I didn't even realize I was standing on the thing. If part of my job is to stay abreast of trends, think about trends in a critical way, and then merge that work into writing and share it with others, what did ChatGPT mean for my future? The future that started as that little girl?

On the drive back from Stillwater, I decided I needed to dig deep. Understanding things is important to me. I needed to better understand AI/ML but also what that meant for the data industry. So many conversations I had up to that point felt like theory, or smoke and mirrors. Depending on who you talk to, AI can be a savior or the beginning of the end. Most of the people I talked with up to this point were in the data industry. From those conversations, it was clear to me that very few people understood the mechanisms of AI. Those that did seem to understand couldn't explain what it does or why it has such power over our future.

I had to pull my head out of the sand (or maybe somewhere else) and buckle down. If this thing was going to swipe away my career, I sure as hell wanted to know when and how. What I found surprised me. It was interesting and exhilarating to learn something so new. There was promise, not only peril. Many people—smart, capable, and ethical people were on watch. But what became obvious to me was that the data industry in which I have spent my career was ill-prepared. My rant that day in Stillwater included a casual warning, "The next 3-5 years in the data industry is going to be a dumpster fire." For once in my life, I don't want to be right.

There was one last piece of the puzzle missing. Since writing "Disrupting Data Governance" (DDG), I've spent a lot of time researching disruption. For many years (even before writing DDG), I had categories I would place people in when I was working with them. It helped me communicate better with them. Since researching disruption, I have refined those categories to full-blown profiles. I often thought about writing that book. But it needed something, a thesis, or theme, a precipitating event. Cue AI.

So, here I am. Writing a book that I never thought I'd write. It's not so much about AI as it is about what happens when something so revolutionary happens in real-time. What happens when FOMO overrides logic? What happens when we brush aside our known standards without a second thought? It's so easy to roll your eyes at the person who says, "But that's how we've always done it!" But in this statement lies a truth. A story worth keeping of hard-fought lessons won. I don't think we should dismiss them. Not only that, but to make this disruption sustainable, we must embrace them.

One

What this is, What it is not

The balance I need to strike is providing enough information about AI so you feel well informed. But not so detailed that you feel like you could finish a PhD dissertation on obscure elements of machine learning (ML) and artificial intelligence (AI). Oddly, at least for this topic, it's a hard balance to strike, unless you've been embedded with the research happening in the big tech companies and certain universities for the last several decades. The sudden, shocking introduction of ChatGPT may have caught you by surprise.

So much of what has been written about AI seems to indicate that it's still decades away. But happening right now is a talent war for anyone who knows anything about deep learning neural networks and machine learning. Salary ranges for these genuine experts are in the mid-range of six figures! There are books on Amazon written exclusively by ChatGPT. It is happening all around us, this revolutionary change, in real time. The proverbial cat is out of the bag, and we are all just trying to catch up without getting clawed to death. I decided my first order of business was to ground myself in what these terms actually mean.

Somewhere among all the noise is logic. I can't help but think about the role our current world view has on the sudden proliferation of AI. The focus on capitalism has made it uncouth and often ill-advised to worry about doing the "right" thing. If you stop and do the right thing, the next start-up will happily skip right past you to the bank. It is difficult to be a leader right now. To know what to do in the face of a technology that, according to both the well- and ill-informed alike, is an existential threat. It's hard to brag about stock prices as the world burns at your feet.

My pessimism needed no encouragement during research for this book. Creating a balanced view of the current situation requires me to quiet that devil on my shoulder and take a deeper look at the spaces between the hype and reality. The hype of sci-fi and alarmists, optimists, pessimists, think tanks, and Big Tech. From that hype, we must build salient guidance for the *people* caught between.

I've thought for years that the "best practices" often touted in the tech and data industries are too narrow. I sometimes wonder who they are "best" for. Best practices designed by large companies don't deploy well to small companies or start-ups. Best practices that are created from dynamic start-up cultures can't scale to large enterprises. As I looked at the current data landscape, I saw no best practices or better practices. Nary a set of reasonable advice for organizations that want to thoughtfully understand AI better.

"Be in the business of creating possibilities for greatness. Innovate or die, and there's no innovation if you operate out of fear of the new or untested."

Bob Iger, Ride of a Lifetime

I will focus quite a bit of my content on the data industry. It's where I've spent the last 25 years and where I feel most capable of providing salient advice. That said, I believe that the research I've done on disruption is applicable to all industries and business units. You can find that content in chapters four and five. While this book is about the current state of our world in the context of AI, the only thing that I can say for certain is that disruption is the order of the day. That feeling you get when you scroll your favorite social media is right after FOMO and right before terror, the sense that nothing is the same and the pace is impossible to keep up with—that's disruption at scale. It is here to stay. There's no waiting around to make sure that people are willing to adopt. You cannot innovate (or disrupt) from fear, though. I would contend that you can't do much from a place of fear, so the intention here is to give you tools to lead, but also to navigate as an individual.

Before we get too far into the content, I want to address the "why me" question. Maybe you're not asking that, but I did. Why is a data consultant weighing in on disruption? While doing research, I noted that most of the books I read that covered this topic were written by people with a big education from fancy schools. Many had a background in management consulting or executive coaching. Admittedly, despite my personal affinity for disruption as I began to write this book, I had a big case of imposter syndrome. Seriously, who do I think I am?

Here's how I answered that. I have spent the last 25 years on the cusp of one of the biggest, disruptive, staggering changes that has happened to business since the Industrial Revolution. Data. Now, data has heralded yet another disruptive change, AI. I've seen disruption and change *from the inside*. I've been on the front lines, selling the "change" that data brought. Helping people navigate challenging situations for their own personal reasons. I've seen companies thrive and grow and companies crash and burn.

The first order of business is to share some information about AI and machine learning. We also have to get past generic references to "AI." Using ChatGPT, or even GenAI, interchangeably with AI, is a bit like describing all motor vehicles by only ever referencing the Honda Civic. It's not helpful and creates more confusion in the long run.

Because I believe that we have to understand history to not repeat it, we will take a quick look back at how we got here with AI. We will also look at what is happening in the marketplace today. I'll make several recommendations for books, articles, blogs, and podcasts as well. The intention here is to give you a baseline set of knowledge. Innovation is happening at a break-neck speed. Anything I write now (end of 2023) will be desperately outdated upon publication of the book, slated for mid-year 2024. While innovation is happening fast, the foundations for AI were set decades ago. Philosophical arguments will continue. For our purposes, we need to understand the basics of AI. To prepare us to lead our organizations through these next volatile years.

The chapters will include how to create sustainable disruption and some sage advice from AI "veterans." Those folks who have spent time building algorithms and working with different AI technologies can guide organizations on how to best position themselves for the next several years. The final section will include a framework for starting your AI journey. Then, we will navigate the questions of value to the organization against spending and responsible AI.

I hope that this book will be more than a guide. My sincere hope is that it serves as a call to action. To better lead our organizations and the people in them. And for all of us to think critically, stay above the fray, and move confidently into the future.

Just for Fun

Throughout this book, I will often use song titles and lyrics to emphasize my point. Think of them like easter eggs and share them with me on social media. I cover most genres, so extra points for obscurity. Follow us @moxyanalytics on LinkedIn and Instagram, and use #spotthesong. See you out there!

Two

Let's Get it Started!

There is no shortage of information about AI, and that's part of the problem. In my research, knowing what to read, watch, and refer to was difficult. There are insanely optimistic viewpoints on AI. On the other hand, some texts alert us to the existential threat of AI. Right now, those extremes seem to be all the easily available content, particularly on social media. Like any pendulum, we will swing back and forth between those two for a while. The truth, as it always is, appears to be somewhere in the middle. I can't tell you exactly what you need to know about AI to run your team. Only you can know that. And there's no way I could write a book that informs you about AI enough to make you feel prepared. That's a much longer book and probably written by someone who knows much more about AI than I do. However, I can impart what I have learned during my research and describe it in the context of traditional data and analytics teams.

What I know for sure is that how we run our data and analytics teams will have to change. It doesn't have to change tomorrow, and for some of us, it will be years before it catches up, but change is inevitable. Let's understand why.

A Brief History Lesson

I'd like to tell you that not everyone needs AI, but it is a temporal truth. How fast that changes depends on several factors. To understand those factors, we have to understand AI. This chapter will be a brief review of not only artificial intelligence but also machine learning. The popular media conflates these broad umbrella terms. In reality, it is several distinct areas of what is generally called "AI." For months, I read and interviewed people on this topic, but it was by no means an exhaustive review. If you feel like you have a decent grip on the concepts of AI, feel free to skip this part. Now, let's dive in.

Saying you're researching AI is a little like saying you're researching medicine. Too general and not helpful. I've always enjoyed research, but with a deadline looming, I knew I needed to have a plan. I focused on three big areas. First, a general understanding of AI. I read books and talked with people who could help break down the concepts into bite-sized nuggets. Second, governance, ethics, and responsible AI. Finally, a deeper dive into the concepts that brought AI and our data teams together. That included knowledge graphs, the semantic web, and frameworks to deploy AI. In the Appendix, I've listed the books that I used and/or referenced. In addition, because I do not consider myself an expert, I use footnotes when referencing specific content.

Concepts of AI, even the term artificial intelligence, was coined in the 1950s.[1] A couple of decades went by with some philosophizing, and in the 70s, things really started to take hold. It was the era of early concepts of the internet and post-space travel, where everything felt possible. It was also the decade when Douglas Hofstadter[2] was working in the exhilarating field of AI. Despite nearly two decades of work, he felt the big dreams of AI were still possible. The dream was about "Creating machines with human-like intelligence," and Hofstadter claimed it was "a profound intellectual adventure..."[3] While these concepts seemed too sci-fi to be real, the foundational aspects of what we consider to be AI started then. You know what really kicked things off? "Big data." Do you know what started the era of big data? The internet. Tracking every little thing we do online spooled up billions of data points that, when strung together, became the spiderweb for AI.

From the Oxford Dictionary comes a definition of "Artificial Intelligence":

---

[1] https://www.forbes.com/sites/gilpress/2016/12/30/a-very-short-history-of-artificial-intelligence-ai/?sh=127b9cbd6fba.

[2] https://en.wikipedia.org/wiki/Douglas_Hofstadter.

[3] Mitchell, M. 2019. Artificial Intelligence: A Guide for Thinking Humans.

"The theory and development of computer systems able to perform tasks that normally require human intelligence, such as visual perception, speech recognition, decision-making, and translation between languages."

Interestingly enough, this doesn't seem to capture much about what I see AI to be in the content I've read. It is a modern version of the definition, to be sure, one that helps encapsulate the progress that has been made on these fronts as part of the LLMs (large language models). I was curious: what would ChatGPT say about it...

Me: "How do you define artificial intelligence?"

Chat:[4]

Artificial Intelligence (AI) refers to the development of computer systems or software that can perform tasks that typically require human intelligence. These tasks include learning, reasoning, problem-solving, perception, understanding natural language, and even the ability to interact with the environment. AI systems aim to mimic or simulate human cognitive functions in order to execute complex functions and adapt to changing circumstances.

There are two main types of AI:

Narrow AI (Weak AI): This type of AI is designed and trained for a particular task. It excels in performing specific functions, but its abilities are limited to the predefined scope. Examples include virtual personal

---

[4] 12/12/2023.

assistants, image recognition software, and recommendation systems.

General AI (Strong AI): This is a more advanced form of AI that possesses the ability to understand, learn, and apply knowledge across diverse tasks, similar to human intelligence. Achieving true general AI is a complex and challenging goal, and as of my last knowledge update in January 2022, it has not been fully realized.

AI can be further categorized into two approaches:

Symbolic AI (Good Old-Fashioned AI or GOFAI): This approach involves using predefined rules and symbols to represent knowledge and solve problems. It relies on explicit programming and is often rule-based.

Machine Learning (ML): This is a subfield of AI that focuses on developing algorithms that allow systems to learn from data. Instead of being explicitly programmed, these systems improve their performance over time as they are exposed to more data. Deep learning, a subset of machine learning, involves neural networks with multiple layers (deep neural networks).

AI has applications in various domains, including healthcare, finance, education, robotics, natural language processing, and more. The field continues to evolve rapidly, with ongoing research and development contributing to its advancements.

It is so much easier to say less with more words than fewer words, and that certainly seems to be the case for ChatGPT. Ask a simple question and get a page-long answer. But to be fair, this answer is far more accurate according to my research than the simple definition offered by Oxford in a Google search. They may start out similarly, but rather than focusing on a few narrow aspects of AI, such as visual perception and speech recognition, the definition from ChatGPT does a much better job of representing the totality of the work: an attempt to mimic humans.

Also included in the ChatGPT version is a definition of machine learning, one that often gets lost in the flurry of excitement towards AI (or Artificial General Intelligence, AGI). Much has been said about ML, or more accurately, much has been said about AI when they actually meant ML. The parts of machine learning that represent "deep learning" or the "deep neural networks" are what cause a lot of concern because if you ask the AI developer to explain what they are doing, she often can't. Why? Well, here lies decades of research, obscure statistical models, billions of rows of data, and you doomscrolling.

Data, Data Everywhere

Do you know what you were doing on April 30, 1993[5]? I was in class, Art History, I think. It was a Friday class, not sure what I was thinking. Anyway, that's the day the internet went online and became available to the general public. It was an exciting idea to connect everyone in the

---

[5] https://www.npr.org/2023/04/30/1172276538/world-wide-web-internet-anniversary#:~:text=Embedded-
,The%20World%20Wide%20Web%20became%20available%20to%20the%20b
roader%20public,with%20graphics%2C%20audio%20and%20hyperlinks.

world via a gossamer-like thread of cable. The nineties were a heady time. We all thought everything would be wonderful forever, the budget was balanced, online shopping was a thing, and hemlines were short (then long, then short again). The internet laid the groundwork for big data— it was exactly what AI needed to take hold.

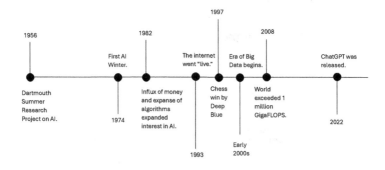

Figure 2.1: History of AI.

Once the internet was up and running, we started to create tiny digital crumbs. In the 90s, they didn't mean anything because we didn't have the computing power to store those crumbs. We all went happily along, searching on Alta Vista. Of course, we're all familiar with Moore's Law. As computational power doubled every few years, by 2000, we started to see gains in computation, which meant we could store more data inexpensively. As exponential growth does, just eight years later, in 2008, the world exceeded one million gigaFLOPS.[6] Taken independently, none of these things seem all that interesting. Perhaps a few funny facts

---

[6] https://ourworldindata.org/moores-law#:~:text=The%20computational%20capacity%20of%20computers,years%2C%20from%201975%20to%202009.&text=More%20recent%20data%20is%20shown,supercomputer%20in%20any%20given%20year.

to spout at a dinner party, so you sound smart. I mean, anyone who can use the word gigaFLOPS in a sentence wins my vote. But these things together, the internet online with millions of users, enough computing power to store their activities, and the increasing sophistication of machine learning algorithms laid the groundwork for AI. All it needed was a little incentive, and it found it in social media, or perhaps more specifically, the companies and stockholders of social media.

Once Upon a Time in a Place Called Silicon Valley

Money changes everything,[7] and these companies got great at keeping us online, greedily grabbing all those digital crumbs you left behind. Those crumbs were fed into these ML algorithms. This is why today, when you ask ChatGPT to explain World War II in teenager parlance, it can answer with shocking accuracy (including adding way too many "likes" and words like "epic"). In the definition above, ChatGPT referenced "narrow AI," and that was what was primarily being built in these early days of the internet, social media, and supercomputers. Using our data to train models, ML would create visual perception algorithms for systems to translate handwriting to text, or seamlessly identify and tag your aunt in a holiday picture, for example. Narrow functions, not expansive or multi-layered

---

[7] Lauper, C. 1983. Money Changes Everything.

functions. Narrow AI just does one thing. To build these narrow capabilities, AI researchers used images gained on Flickr, and broke them down, pixel by pixel, so they could identify what was in them.

As you might recall from your college statistics class, you needed lots of data to gain power in an algorithm or formula. The more data, the more power. AI researchers would take these pictures and, using "supervised learning" concepts, break each pixel down to binary code, whether something was in the pixel or not. The "supervised" part was a person helping the algorithm understand that any shade of gray meant *yes*, and any shade of not gray meant *no*. These are called "labeled data sets," and something similar was happening across several different types of AI, making everything binary to mimic human responses.

What is Data?

When I say "data" in reference to ChatGPT, LLMs, or even AI, I am actually referencing text (or sometimes images or audio). The vast majority of the world's data is actually in these unstructured or semi-structured formats. That's the challenge AI is solving: taking these data types and making them easier for machines to understand. Most software or algorithms easily consume numerical data. That's not where the magic is.

Over time, scale became an issue. To achieve true AGI, supervised learning was never going to cut it. They (the AI researchers and developers) needed to let the machines cull through the billions of rows of data (i.e., text). "Unsupervised learning refers to a broad group of methods for learning categories or actions without labeled data."[8] Letting the machines learn from billions of rows of our data, creating layers of "hidden units" as part of the neural networks, is where AI starts to get scary. Some of the most compelling possibilities of AI exist in millions of layers of deep neural networks (DNN) that are not explainable to or by a human. That screeching sound you hear right now? That's AI going off the rails.

Hallucinations in Generative AI (the type of AI that accounts for ChatGPT, among others) account for about 20% of the results.[9] We all heard in 2023 about the lawyer who had ChatGPT write his brief, only to find out that it was all fake. While it's concerning, it is not surprising. Most generative AI (unsupervised) models are built using predictive algorithms. From the trillions of rows of data (text), they use statistics to determine how often words appear together. Those are word pairs. Researchers got stuck there for a while. Then, they realized that it's about the overall context, not just the next word. That led them to word vectors.[10] Imagine placing words related to each other on multiple axes based on how often you've seen them together, say in social media data. Draw a box on a white board, then start to place words and word pairs

---

[8] Mitchell, M. 2019. Artificial Intelligence: A Guide for Thinking Humans.

[9] https://www.datanami.com/2023/01/17/hallucinations-plagiarism-and-chatgpt/.

[10] Direction as well as magnitude
https://www.techtarget.com/whatis/definition/vector#:~:text=A%20vector%20is%20a%20quantity,force%2C%20electromagnetic%20fields%20and%20weight.

where words like "resignation letter" might be close to each other on two (or more) axes. I'll give you a real-life example that I lived through. I started teaching a course called "Committee-free Data Governance." I decided I needed to gamify the experience of what it's like to have committees in the middle of every little decision. I created an "escape game," which required me to make or build a bunch of little things to make the situation feel more real. I wanted to write an angry resignation letter from a data steward. For most of the things like this, I used ChatGPT because it was a lot of content to write. So, I anticipated that ChatGPT would easily be able to handle an angry resignation letter from a data steward. It turns out that those things did not work out together. Now I know that these predictive algorithms likely did not have *angry*, *data steward*, and *resignation letter* together. I could easily find a resignation letter; I could even get one from a data steward. I could also get an angry resignation letter. What I could not do was get an angry resignation letter from a data steward.

These formulas are not built on (supervised) context, and, as we know, anybody can say anything on the internet. All these systems are doing, and quite well, I might add, is predicting the next word. Certainly, "hallucinations" or errors, are par for the course. The trouble isn't that people don't expect errors. The trouble is we can't always explain them. That's because those hidden units, or deep neural networks, can be millions of units, and it's not just one "unit" or package of code that leads to hallucinations, it's several. To create complex responses to simple questions from binary data (text turned into machine-readable code), you have to have many layers (we're talking millions). This is one of the reasons why advocates for responsible AI talk about explain-ability in the code.[11] If the programmer who created it can't explain why it happened, what chance do any of us have?

Researching AI elicited a lot of emotional reactions in me. I was in awe at the sheer tenacity of thinking we could create a machine that mimics cognition. I was curious why so many disciplines were involved (everything from psychology and neurology to artists and musicians)—decades, often entire careers of professors and researchers, dedicated to the task. But what really got us here, on the cusp of Artificial General Intelligence, is capitalism. As a theoretical exercise, we would never be this far if the only value was to see if we could store our brains Dr. Zola style.[12] Capitalism will push the data and analytics industry faster towards AI than we're comfortable with. Faster than we are ready for.

"It took me 66 years to become an overnight sensation"

AI

---

[11] https://www.whitehouse.gov/ostp/ai-bill-of-rights/notice-and-explanation/.

[12] https://marvelcinematicuniverse.fandom.com/wiki/Arnim_Zola#:~:text=In%20the%20comics%2C%20Arnim%20Zola,evokes%20his%20comic%2Dbook%20counterpart.

Not All Data is Equal

The current popularity of AI was heralded by ChatGPT. This exciting tool seems almost mythical in its capabilities, but we know that it's not. What it did do was get everyone talking. This summer, I was sitting at the dinner table with my 90-year-old father, and my aunt and uncle who are in their 80s, listening to them explain AI. You can overhear it at the grocery store or beauty salon, on the bus, or in a bar. It is everywhere. And for someone who has spent their entire career in a data field, it was shocking to hear people casually discuss complex functions (sometimes accurately) that for so long had been fodder for the few.

Despite the "magic" of LLMs, I could not determine the impact that they would have on your average data repository.[13] Certainly, organizations can use ChatGPT to write marketing blurbs or even code, but LLMs are built on unstructured data,[14] not the typical structured data that lives in data repositories. For that, we need semantic layers. Think of a semantic[15] layer as a translation layer between you and all of those bits and bytes (literal ones and zeros) of information.

---

[13] I use the generic term "data repository" to encapsulate any reference to data warehouses, data lakes, data lake houses, etc.

[14] Actually, LLMs can be built using structured data, they just have to deconstruct it first, make it words or...add the semantics of data.

[15] Definition: Of meaning, especially meaning of language. Found in my 1983 version of Webster's Unabridged Dictionary, page 1648.

We have talked about semantic layers for as long as I can remember. In the 2000s, people built these fictional semantic layers using data governance functions (fictional because they rarely succeeded at doing what they intended). They were, at least theoretically, meant to be a translation layer, but a lot got lost in translation. The trouble came in the complexity. For the 1990s and most of the 2000s, how you architected your data mattered a lot. The commercially available options for high computational power didn't exist (and the cloud was just something up in the sky). The only way you could guarantee performance and volume was to carefully architect your data. As these supercomputers (i.e., powerful servers) became more generally available, organizations started to worry less about architecture because the sheer power of the machines could make up for poorly architected data (such as too many joins).

Then came the trouble of lots of data with not a lot of context nor how to use it. Semantic layers became all the rage. It meant defining everything in your "warehouse" so anyone could use anything. It was the core of what "business intelligence" was supposed to offer, "the right data at the right time to the right person in the right way." But it never happened that way—even if technology could do it. The formality of creating the definitions and metadata required for semantic layers was too much for most organizations. Under the banner of data governance, organizations attempted to create standard terms. It seemed like defining your words for consistency, so everyone knew what a customer was, for example, would be easy. But because we tried to define terms for many different uses, often politics got in the way of data governance and semantic layers paid the price.

Modern semantic layers have a leg up. Using the concepts of data catalogs, terms are crowd-sourced and weighted. Knowledge graphs[16] bring together LLMs and structured data. It's a contextually driven, crowd-sourced semantic layer that can use structured and unstructured data. While an LLM doesn't necessarily require knowledge graphs to interact with a structured data set, it does improve accuracy.[17] Now, before you run out and start implementing knowledge graphs, it's important to note that these are the early days of commercializing AI. No doubt, more solutions will become available over time.

Knowledge graphs do seem to solve the rather specific question of how much LLMs can help with enterprise solutions. But the bigger questions are, "What solves the problem of using the systems we've already built?" and "How can we do that in a safe, ethical, and fiscally responsible way?" Again, knowledge graphs do seem to offer a solution. It is the one way your organization builds an ontology (so you're in charge) and connects all data types.

---

[16] https://ai.stanford.edu/blog/introduction-to-knowledge-graphs/.

[17] https://ai.plainenglish.io/new-research-proves-knowledge-graphs-drastically-improve-accuracy-of-large-language-models-on-0f1dbcc08d61.

Speed and Scale

I often joke that AI is like me with too much coffee—it just helps do dumb stuff faster. But when you look at the considerations of AI for our enterprises, understanding the speed and scale these systems offer is paramount. The potential to disrupt every aspect of our data teams is not a joke. I'm not usually the one pumping the brakes. But I do believe that it is critical that we, at least, downshift right now to better understand the implications before we light this thing on fire. In some cases, once you start, you can't go back. Let's at least walk into this with our eyes wide open.

I'll admit that after all these years, it's exciting to think about so much value coming from data repositories across many enterprises. Using AI and ML to do everything from creating crowd-sourced definitions to ML algorithms solving pesky data quality problems. Someday, you'll be able to ask a question in text form and get a response both in narrative as well as graphically. I can see myself sitting quietly in my home library, retired from an exciting career in data. It might be a bit premature to call my financial advisor. Yes, there is no doubt that we are on the cusp of a few wild years in the data industry. The degree of insanity is actually up to you and your peers. I know you don't want to feel left out, and the pressure to be future-ready is overwhelming. We owe it to ourselves and to our teams to step back for a hot minute and consider what these (so far) narrow AI solutions offer us, what options we have for linking them together, and the implications for the people who report to us. Not only is the speed and scale something to be wary of before you get started, we must understand the responsible and ethical use of these systems.

Let's Not do Dumb Stuff Faster

Ethics is a big field. I'll admit that when I started this research, what I knew about ethics, specifically tech and data ethics, could fit in a thimble. I've always been an advocate, but the truth is that it was easier for me to say, "That's important, we should do something about that," and then make references to the work of other people. It's a position of privilege to do that, and after researching, I know now that accountability lies with all of us.

When students become doctors, they take an oath to first "Do No Harm." When you think about it, that's great because doctors have your life in their hands. The scale of harm a doctor can inflict in a lifetime is *minuscule* compared to the impact AI systems may have on the average population. Yet, we think nothing of holding a doctor to a higher standard. They take that oath; the medical industry is set up to ensure that they hold each other accountable. There is a post-mortem review called a morbidity and mortality conference (M&M for short) if a doctor causes harm. The doctor can be removed from practice. In other words, the medical industry is set up to monitor the impact.

Airline pilots have a code of ethics,[18] and we all expect them to take that seriously. They don't get drunk or high and then fly a couple hundred people around. My point here is that when there are professions that have an impact on human life, we expect those professions to follow standards of ethics. We expect consequences for those actions when the worst happens. One could argue that there is a clear cause and effect for doctors and pilots. If they take an action that causes harm, such as death, the ethical standards as set by their profession step in and investigate. Punitive action is taken if ethics are violated. As a society, we expect that when someone causes harm in such a direct way, they are held accountable. But AI is part of a complicated world. There is no obvious cause and effect. The harm that the models may cause is not as obvious as death. But passing the buck or refusing to hold people accountable for the harm they do because it's a more obscured path will result in dire consequences.

In the world of data privacy and information security, there's a concept of "first line of defense," or FLOD[19] for short. It refers to the idea that there are layers or steps to prevent some, if not all, of the bad stuff that happens to enterprise systems via "bad actors" (hackers, not the people that get Razzies). One could argue that in the world of tech and data, particularly where the intent is a large audience (i.e., software systems or algorithms aimed at gaining

---

[18] https://www.alpa.org/en/about-alpa/what-we-do/code-of-ethics.

[19] https://www.isaca.org/resources/isaca-journal/issues/2018/volume-4/roles-of-three-lines-of-defense-for-information-security-and-governance#:~:text=Briefly%2C%20the%20first%20line%20of,facilitate%20the%20management%20of%20risk.

market share for their shareholders), the minimum we should ask for is the multi-layered approach to lines of defense or accountability.

Today, there is a big gap between the tech industry's approach to creating software and algorithms and their impact on individuals, enterprises, and systems (i.e., governments). Allowing these organizations, big or small, to unleash algorithms with untold impact with little more than a pithy mantra to not do bad stuff is naïve at best.

Kwality is Job One

I like cars. I don't *love* cars, it's not like I'm a gearhead (that's my son), but I've always appreciated fast, beautiful cars. Growing up in the 1980s, there was some folklore surrounding certain brands of cars. Back then, there were not as many brands as there are today. For example, Ford was an acronym (according to some) that stood for "Found On Road Dead" or "Fix Or Repair Daily."[20] So prolific was the quality issue that Ford started a public advertising campaign to address these issues. Proudly exclaiming, long before they had a right to, "Ford, Quality is Job One." What followed was, surprisingly, an increase in quality. It wasn't an overnight revelation. I owned a 1990 Ford Escort that was far from a high-quality car. In 1999, everything was wrong with it when I traded it in. I drove that thing with a

---

[20] https://www.forbes.com/sites/larrylight/2019/05/28/im-ford-and-im-proud/?sh=5a7050784f1c.

broken head gasket for two years (I got tired of repairing it), a broken speedometer, door handles that didn't work, body trim flapping as I drove down the highway...you get the idea. Intention is like that. If you publicly state your intention, someone will hold you accountable. And over time, Ford stopped being the punchline for jokes and became (again) an innovative car company.

Data quality kept coming up in my research on AI. Depending on who you talk to, you will get a variety of responses from "Don't worry about quality, the machines will figure it out," to "If you don't worry about quality, the machines will never figure it out." First, let me just say that we are nowhere near where machines can determine the quality of our data. We may get there. I posited in "Disrupting Data Governance" that with enough data ML algorithms should easily be able to detect outliers to be brought to the attention of a responsible adult. I still stand by that. But that doesn't give organizations a free pass to not worry about data quality. As a matter of fact, for those who are experimenting with AI and using publicly available models, the data you put in it really matters. A lot. Customizing LLMs using the base models means you're probably using structured data from your repository, among other things.

To start your AI journey, most organizations will begin with point solutions. That is, AI that comes packaged in other software. To fine tune these models, this software will access your data (preferably in the cloud; more on that later), which means that it's *your* data. Be honest with yourself. With everything that you know about AI right now, would you feel good about plugging AI algorithms into your existing data? The less data you use (for example, to customize a GenAI model), the more important the quality of that data is. GenAI models are built on millions, if not billions, of rows of data. If you're personalizing one, such as the experiment Moxy did to create a "Laura-Bot" to answer questions about data governance, the data you use to personalize has to be good to ensure that personalization is spot on. We used all the blogs, books, and presentations I'd written to make sure the "Laura-Bot" answered questions in the way that I would. It worked because the relatively small amount of data that we used had all been edited and pressure tested.

One critically important note before we get too far. Data quality, as we've thought about it in the data industry, is not the same as data quality as we will come to think about it. These base models that feed things like ChatGPT are based mostly on text, which is why we hear so many conflicting opinions about the quality of your data. The way we have historically thought about data quality in the data industry has been focused on structured data. It was possible for us to create mathematical equations to test that data. For much of what we know today as "AI", specifically GenAI, is based on text. Testing text for accuracy is different than testing numbers. The algorithms can use structured, unstructured, or semi-structured data, though, which is why data quality will continue to be important.

In the last twenty-five years of my career, I can name about five companies that took data quality seriously. Five. In twenty-five years. That's abysmal but true. To be fair, my selection criteria are skewed because if you're calling me for help, you are probably missing things. But this isn't just about those companies that I worked with. It's also about companies that I was aware of. We all like to talk about data quality, but the work on data quality seems just out of reach.

The international organization DAMA (data management association) published in 2009 the Data Management Body of Knowledge,[21] known as DMBOK (pronounced like mmm-Bop but with a "D" at the start and a "K" at the end. Now you have that song in your head, you're welcome). The DMBOK defined dimensions of data quality: Completeness, Consistency, Conformity, Accuracy, Integrity, and Timeliness. Now, when you Google "dimensions of data quality," some variation of these six dimensions is usually included. I would contend, however, that as we all start to dip our toes into the AI pool, these six dimensions are not enough. Some of the challenges are operational, such as the amount of data. You can't claim high-quality data when you have a couple hundred rows, can you? What about the diversity of data? When it comes to LLMs and the vectors they build using predictive models, the more variety you have in the data you feed it, the more realistic it feels. A much more expansive set of data quality dimensions is included in "Executing Data Projects: Ten Steps to Quality Data and Trusted Information," by Danette McGilvray. In her text, she includes fourteen dimensions and allows for other dimensions that are organization specific.

Danette McGilvray's Data Quality Dimensions:

1. Perception of Relevance and Trust
2. Data Specifications

---

[21] https://www.dama.org/cpages/body-of-knowledge.

3. Data Integrity Fundamentals
4. Accuracy
5. Uniqueness and Deduplication
6. Consistency and Synchronization
7. Timeliness
8. Access
9. Security and Privacy
10. Presentation Quality
11. Data Coverage
12. Data Decay
13. Usability and Transactability
14. Other Relevant Data Quality Dimensions

If you don't focus on data quality as you start your AI journey, you're being irresponsible. The internet is loaded with examples of what happens when you don't take data quality seriously. As we saw with the Ford example, intention helps set the pace. Don't just put lip-service to it. Build out a team that is dedicated to the task of improving your data quality. It is a journey, without a doubt. One of the reasons why data quality eludes so many organizations is because it feels like such a large effort to undertake. The reality is any stated intention to improve data quality, with a little effort, will improve your data quality. Then, you can confidently go into the future.

Would you like AI with that?

Based on all that is available to read right now, you would think that AI, true AI, is prolific. Certainly, LLMs have taken over the chatbot world. Recommendation engines are all the rage since Amazon has been helping you buy stuff you didn't need. Those engines have continued to improve over time, too. Recently, I was on Amazon getting my tea (decaf Chai) and sunscreen, and up popped into the recommendation section a set of Disney Villains from Barbie. How did they do that?! (And yes, please!)

We're not Amazon, Google, or Microsoft. The question is, what type of AI can most organizations really deploy or use? There is certainly the question of buy or build. There is also a question of feasibility. The one truth is that building AI/ML from scratch needs data, lots and lots of data. The average company doesn't have that much data. You can buy data or create synthetic data, or you can buy the LLM and pump your (smaller) data into it for your purposes. Those all require big investments. If you want to "build" because you have a great idea, you have to find an AI developer, and, last I heard, good ones have a salary that borders on seven figures. While AI can't solve everything, not yet, anyway, there are some real-life limitations to what the average organization can take on, given restraints on time, money, and resources. It is part of the ethical question of AI because today, it seems as if it is only for the hands of the few with deep pockets.

Today, every software package you buy claims to have AI in it. In the last section of this book, we will consider what it takes for an organization of average size to take on an AI project and what is realistic in terms of what you can build versus what you can buy. The danger is thinking you can just buy some software package with AI in it without taking the responsibility to check what it's doing. As we learned earlier, the ability to proliferate bad assumptions at scale with AI is easy, too easy. It is all of our responsibility to approach these projects with a healthy dose of skepticism and a "yes, but" attitude.

But, like, how?!

There's a psychological principle called the "Locus of Control."[22] Maybe you remember it from your college psychology course? It addresses the degree to which you control portions of your environment. In other words, how much you believe you control what happens to you. What does that have to do with AI? Not much, but it does have a lot to do with what you decide are your next steps.

It is hard to take accountability when you play a small role in a bigger game. I don't use the word "game" lightly. In thinking about how to represent systems, organizations, big or small, and the interplay between individuals and these systems or organizations, I think the word "game" is a good fit. For the last four years, I've spent most of my time doing data governance. That happened sort of by accident when I wrote the book "Disrupting Data Governance." In the last four years, I've found that the failure of most organizations to execute data governance can often come down to one thing: they can't get out of their own way. Now, there are a billion reasons why they can't get out of their own way; some of them are legitimate, and some of them are just straight-up politics. Working in an organization that puts

---

[22] https://www.psychologytoday.com/us/basics/locus-control.

barriers between you and doing the right thing makes it difficult to take accountability for your role in anything as big as AI.

If I can get philosophical for a moment, nothing we have created is real. Governments, corporations, money, it's all made up. We made it up to create boundaries, exercise authority, and manage (or control) society. We (as humanity) have given these things power by attributing value to them. That's okay. Not everyone is willing to live in a fast and loose, chaos-loving environment. But sometimes, we forget that we did that, which means that we forget we can undo it. That comes back to the idea of how much control we have over our own systems. At a minimum, we certainly have control over our own actions and decisions (even our feelings, or at least that's what my psychiatrist says).

To take back some of this control, the first thing we have to do is to get better informed. The knowledge and skills, specifically around AI and ML, are right now in the hands of a few. I don't expect you to run out and get a PhD in computer science, but becoming well informed about the function of these systems so we can intelligently and respectfully hold organizations and each other accountable is paramount. If your organization wants to use AI and you're getting a ton of pressure to develop an "AI strategy" but lack the knowledge and skills in your team, then get educated first. The scale and speed at which AI can impact our world is nothing to shrug your shoulders at, and that starts, even in small ways, with how you answer the question, "What is our AI strategy?"

A list of recommended readings is in the Appendix. On the short list (of a rather long list), would be "Artificial Intelligence: A Guide for Thinking Humans" by Melanie Mitchell. "Data Conscience: Algorithmic Siege on our Humanity" by Brandeis Hill Marshall, and follow Elizabeth Adams[23] on social media to learn more about Responsible AI and the real-life actions you can take. Becoming well-informed is the first step to understanding what actions you can take to help your organization sustain the disruption that will be occurring over the next several years.

The tech space has been volatile for several years now. The world has been volatile since time immemorial. What is true today is that it seems we have a front seat to everything, all of it. Historically, the front seat was guaranteed only for what happened in your backyard, and if you were lucky, your backyard was quiet most years. Volatility can stifle critical thinking, creating reactions rather than thoughtful actions. Some people are better at managing that disruption, while some can take it as it is and maybe even optimize it. Others, not so much. The reality is that disruption, or volatility, will be the norm. While corporations struggle to decide what new technologies best suit them, the industry moves on to something more innovative or fashionable. Just when you think LLMs are the wave of the future, somebody starts talking about AGI.

I tend to embrace disruption. I'm good with change and excited to take on new challenges. I also know that that is not true of everyone. The ability to bring everyone with us on this journey into whatever the future holds at your

---

[23] https://eadams.tech/.

organization will be the job of the day for the next few years. Leading the ship through the bumpy waters to be future-ready, whatever that future looks like, will be no easy feat.

The remainder of this book will focus on this exact effort. Today, as I write this, ChatGPT is the current disruptive technology, and we all know that's just the tip of the iceberg. To be truly future-ready means we have to prepare our teams to manage a sustainable amount of disruption. In the next section of this book, we will discover the types of roles every organization needs (and already has) to take the best advantage of disruption rather than feeling steamrolled by new technologies. In the last section, we will dive deep into a pragmatic framework to navigate AI consistently, reliably, and responsibly and whatever comes after it.

Three

Getting Future-Ready: Options and Considerations

While I have a reputation for disrupting things, those who know me well know I have a very pragmatic streak. Perhaps it started in the little farmhouse I grew up in or from years of living in the realities of corporate America. Regardless of its origins, it's important to me to strike the right balance. Sometimes, getting the day-to-day done is hard enough. From the start, I wanted this book to balance the disruptive nature of AI and the reality of what most small- to mid-sized organizations can do.

Future proofing has been a goal for many data systems for the last decade. The idea that you can avoid failure by building something that reduces the likelihood of obsolescence feels like wishful thinking. All technologies and algorithms have a shelf life—somewhere between bread and dried beans. That's true now more than ever. There is no way to be future proof because no one knows what that future might look like. Being future-ready means that we will anticipate but not predict that we are ready for change. Do yourself a big favor and get used to it. We will build into our systems the inevitability of obsolescence. Build teams and methods around deprecating what doesn't work. Don't hold on to stuff just because you think it might work in the future or with enough modifications. Our organizations are moving too fast to double down on what is not working.

Guiding principles are a good way of setting your intentions. I've asked the teams to set their own guiding principles in every organization I've led. When things get difficult, and you're unsure what to do next, the answer is probably somewhere in those principles. This should be a collective exercise—I've started it here for you to get over the tyranny of the blank page.

Guiding Principles

- The ability to be nimble enough to pivot when new technology becomes ready for use.

- The ability to test concepts as well as software, algorithms, or machines, and reject them when they fail to meet our guiding principles.

- The ability to hold yourself and your systems accountable in real-life pressure tests to ensure responsiveness, perform ethically, and guarantee accuracy.

- All data types (structured, unstructured, and semi-structured) are addressed in some capacity.

- The willingness to invest.

- The acknowledgment that the pursuit of knowledge has value, even if there is no deliverable as a result.

- Be good stewards of resources, both people and financial.

- Invest in your people and upskill as a rule.

Truly, the only way to be future-ready is to focus on people and solutions. What solutions look like for our data teams and repositories in the age of AI is still a big question. I had so many conversations with varying experts about what to include. The truth is no one really knows. We're so early in the commercialization of AI that it's hard to know what the future holds. And while I stand behind the theory and principles of what being future-ready means, only time will tell if it holds up. So, as I started to think about what I *specifically* would recommend you consider as part of your solutions, I wanted to use my own set of guiding principles. The first is small budgets. The reality is that most companies can't spend millions of dollars to do this. As a result, that quickly rules out building your own AI from scratch. Also, focusing too much on it violated my second consideration, existing data capabilities. I wanted to guide those organizations that have spent years, sometimes decades, building a data repository. That's not throw-away work. We need to find a way to bring all the data types[24] together. Finally, I wanted to give a couple of options. There is no one-size-fits-all. Too often, we get stuck in that trap. What's right for a multi-national corporation might not work for a small business. What works for a mid-sized company is probably not scalable to a 30,000-employee enterprise.

Balancing all these considerations with high-value add options that vary in complexity and flexibility was the order of the day. No matter where you land with this, know that you will have to pick your own version of difficulty. It is all difficult and not doing anything is difficult, too, because of the pressure that exists today. Doing something is difficult because if you're doing it, you should do it well.

Here's where I landed:[25] knowledge graphs, point solutions, or a hybrid approach. I'll explain each, but let's take a moment to consider your decision points. Things that should be on top of the list:

1. Budget
2. Timeline
3. Skills

What is your budget? Do you know what your organization is willing to invest? Be realistic. You can't help yourself if you try to tackle AI without a financial commitment from your organization. What is your timeline? Do you have

---

[24] Structured (what is in most data repositories), unstructured (think text) and semi-structured (a mix).

[25] These are by no means the only options.

executives or your board of directors breathing down your neck to "do AI"? Maybe no one is asking, but you know it's coming. Either way, understanding how much time you have to commit to any AI strategy or effort is important to know. Finally, what skills does your team or organization already have? Think not only about your capabilities but also your organizational maturity. Not all of these will be equal. If you have some incredible resources and a lot of time, your budget isn't as important. If you have few resources but a giant bucket of money, well, good for you!

Knowledge Graphs

Most digital native companies use proprietary knowledge graphs. I even mentioned it earlier in this book. The description of knowledge graphs goes something like this:

"...a structured representation of knowledge that captures relationships between entities and their attributes. It is a way to organize and connect information in a manner that reflects the real-world relationships and semantics of data. Knowledge graphs are used to model knowledge in a format that is both human-readable and machine-understandable." -ChatGPT

They've been around for a while and have proven to be very effective. Knowledge graphs, by design, solve the challenges of context, access controls, conceptual reuse, and traceability (among others). They are a powerful option in this context because they can use any data type. Google uses knowledge graphs for maps. Amazon uses knowledge graphs for Alexa's question-and-answer service. Smaller organizations could use knowledge graphs to combine their CRM with supply chain and social media data to create a powerful customer portal. There are a few things about knowledge graphs that led me to include them as an option.

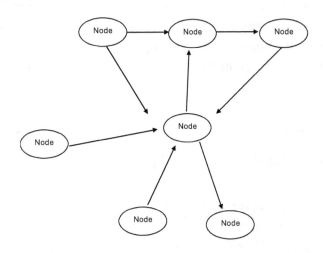

Figure 3.1: Visual Representation of a Knowledge Graph.

First, they bridge data types. Knowledge graphs contextualize data by representing entities and the relationships between them. This method helps in organizing information that might be inherently unstructured or semi-structured. They also provide context to unstructured data. By capturing relationships and context, knowledge graphs add a layer of meaning to unstructured data. They help interpret and link disparate pieces of information, providing a more comprehensive understanding. Second, they focus on semantics (through building an ontology), which helps the average person interact with the data. Third, they acknowledge relationships (they don't necessarily define them). The most compelling example of the extensibility of the knowledge graph is described in *Data-Centric Revolution*: "A node might have a dozen arcs radiating out from it. Maybe all the nodes of a certain type also have a dozen arcs radiating out from them. Then, someone makes another assertion about one of the nodes. Now one of them has thirteen arcs radiating out."

At the end of the day, knowledge graphs make it easier to query and analyze all data types, enabling users to explore relationships and patterns within the information. The benefit compared to traditional models that we have historically used in data repositories is with a knowledge graph, we do not need to know the structure of the data ahead of time.[26] This is valuable for extracting insights from both structured and unstructured data sources.

That doesn't mean they're without challenges. For one thing, you still have to build them. The ontology alone will be a challenge. If you've never stored unstructured data before, you will want to do that to take full advantage of knowledge graph capabilities. Creating these will require new skills and more alignment with the business (to help with the semantic part of those ontologies). Be warned, organizational inertia, or as the folks at Semantic Arts call it, technology incongruence is a real risk. "It diverts resources from business goals, extends time-to-value, leads

---

[26] "Data Centric Revolution" Dave McComb. Page 150.

to business frustration, and inhibits an organization's ability to automate operational processes."[27]

Point-Solutions

A point solution is software that solves a specific use case using AI. On the scale of flexibility, point solutions don't exactly win big. But where they do have an advantage is with ease (well, there's a nuance) and business value. Focusing on point solution options like Dataiku, Databricks, or DataRobot[28] allows your organization to dip your toe into AI. Delivering value one use case at a time and allowing your organization to define what success means. With enough money, you could probably have several point solutions that will get you reasonably far.

If you stick with a couple of trusted vendors, it won't be *too* much of a logistical nightmare. The downside is that when you have several vendors (which is a likely scenario considering how many vendors claim their software has "AI"), it could become a governance and management nightmare. You run the risk of duplication of use cases, particularly if you have business lines buying software with no enterprise check to see if something like that exists somewhere else in the enterprise. It won't be cheap. Even

---

[27] Steve Case, Data-Centric Ambassador, Semantic Arts.

[28] These are not recommendations; it is an acknowledgement of the type of work these vendors do. I'm not sponsored. If I was, I'd drive a nicer car.

if you're careful not to duplicate use cases, it's easy to spend a lot of money on point solutions. As you scale these one-offs (because that's what they are), you will struggle to keep up with what they do and how they do it. Managing point solutions could be a full-time job.

Hybrid Theory[29]

If you're not keen on building a knowledge graph and point solutions sound a lot like Vegas-style ka-ching, there is one more option: a mixed-bag approach. It is not exactly the best of breed; it is more like a combination of different types of technologies, with some AI, some not, and maybe a few point solutions that will address (very) specific needs in your organization. These "bits and pieces" of technology should be purpose-built. In no scenario should you build stuff with no purpose behind it. As you follow your own future-ready guiding principles, remember to build with obsolescence in mind. Nothing lasts forever.

Manage this hybrid approach like any other part of your data platform. Just because it started as a mixed bag doesn't mean that you leave it that way. One of the most challenging parts of this approach is that your consumers may have to navigate through various types of user

---

[29] https://en.wikipedia.org/wiki/Hybrid_Theory sort of a cheat when I footnote it, I know.

experiences. You will need to ensure that your training methods are up to par.

What might you consider as you create your hybrid? Start by addressing the (typical) gap between unstructured and structured data. That is, look to natural language processing (NLP) text mining or text analytics.

Use NLP techniques to extract structured information from unstructured text. This includes tasks such as named entity recognition (NER), sentiment analysis, and part-of-speech tagging. NLP helps understand and categorize text, making it more amenable to structured analysis. These techniques are becoming more ubiquitous in healthcare. LLMs are replacing NLP. Lower on the complexity score is text analytics or text mining. With these, you can extract information and patterns from text data. Text mining tools can identify key concepts, relationships, and sentiments within large volumes of textual information.

Even if you decide that knowledge graphs aren't your thing, creating ontologies and taxonomies can provide a structured framework for organizing data concepts (nodes) and their relationships (edges). An ontology is "a set of concepts and categories in a subject area or domain that shows their properties and the relationships between them."[30] They help categorize and link entities, providing a more organized and structured view of unstructured data. A taxonomy simply names, describes, and classifies. Together, ontologies and taxonomies codify the concepts

---

[30] Google search 5/30/2024, Oxford dictionary definition.

so that more people can navigate the information. I like to think about them like scaffolding.

If you're feeling prepared to dip your toe into machine learning (ML), you can train models to classify and categorize unstructured data based on patterns and features. This approach is useful for automatically structuring information, especially in areas like document classification and content tagging.

If you've been around for a while, you know that data wrangling, data engineering, or ETL (Extract, Transform, Load) are common ways to transform data into useful information. Data wrangling involves the process of cleaning, structuring, and organizing data for analysis. ETL tools transform unstructured data into a structured format suitable for storage and analysis in databases or data warehouses. Combined with data integration platforms, you can combine diverse data sources, including all data types, formats, and structures.

You could use both graph databases and semantic web technologies as part of your hybrid approach, particularly if you've built some ontologies or taxonomies. Graph databases are particularly well-suited for scenarios where relationships play a crucial role, allowing for the creating of a connected data model. Semantic web technologies, such as RDF (Resource Description Framework), are often used for product offerings on websites and OWL (Web Ontology Language),[31] which is an ontology "builder" that can build on RDF. They both enable the representation of

---

[31] https://www.w3.org/OWL/.

data in a standardized and semantically rich format. These operate like starter scaffolding. They also excel at interconnectedness because any organization that adapts either of these share basic aspects of the scaffolding. This helps create a common understanding of the data's meaning and relationships.

Data virtualization allows users to access and query data from various sources, regardless of its structure. It provides a unified and virtual view of data, enabling seamless integration and analysis from the source rather than pulling it into a shared location. A good example of data virtualization is dashboards. Companies can use data virtualization at the data consumption layer, creating dashboards from multiple different sources without additional steps of movement or integration.

Regardless of which choice you make, data catalogs should seriously be considered to help organize and catalog diverse datasets, providing metadata and context that facilitate the understanding and integration of both structured and unstructured data. They also help operationalize data governance concepts, which are critical to any solid AI deployment.

Combining these methods based on specific use cases and data characteristics can help organizations bridge the gap between unstructured and structured data, enabling more comprehensive and insightful analysis.

Four

Disruption in Modern Times

In early 2020, I was asked by a local Minneapolis-based software company if I could give a keynote address at their annual developer's conference. I was intrigued by the offer because they wanted me to talk about disruption in a world that was full of it. My book, "Disrupting Data Governance," was published just four months before COVID became a word in our lexicon. I never imagined that disruption would become an integral part of our everyday lives. I had studied disruption for that book and decided it got a bad name. But alas, I was focused on data governance, not the nature of disruption, so until that request in early 2020, I had no real reason to think about it.

To explain how I got to these ideas about disruption, I have to share a personal story that, if I'm being honest, does not paint me in the kindest light. In early 2018, I was bored in my job and boredom for me is a dangerous state. My day-to-day routine had evolved into a series of maintenance tasks. The same thing week after week, including status updates and casual one-on-one meetings. It is the standard for most middle managers in corporate America. But the routine had dulled my senses, and I felt held back, limited, and anxious. I needed a new challenge. If I had the language I have now, I would have channeled this moment into something positive and proactively talked with my leader about my feelings. Instead, I started poking around where I didn't belong.

I instigated an organizational change that, rather than fulfilling my expectations of providing a new challenge, put me in a position of reporting to someone who had no idea what I did. It was the opposite of what I needed, and quite honestly, for where I was in my career, it was a slap in the face. I quit that job, which I should have done when I realized I needed a challenge. The trouble is, I wanted to continue to support the organization. I wanted to be a part of their future.

As I reflected on that situation, I realized it was a repeating pattern. And just like a teenager in the middle of a bad break-up, I insisted it was all their fault and none of mine. But the reality was that the only thing consistent with all these bad break-ups was me. I instigated, poked, prodded, and needled my way into a corner. While full of good intentions, I came off as ungrateful and disrespectful.

This was at the top of my mind when I started thinking about disruption. Although I was embarrassed about how I acted in many of these cases, I was proud of the work I had done until I got bored. Despite several attempts to explain my behavior (therapy, reading, personality assessments), nothing ever resonated with me enough to explain why I loved blowing stuff up. I destroyed professional relationships that were important to me. I threw the baby out with the bathwater because I reached a point where my need to disrupt overwhelmed my want to play nice. To be fair, my want to "play nice" is very low, and even my first-grade teacher commented on it.

When I gave that talk about how organizations can innovate in times of chaos and churn (you know, modern times) while not burning people out, I had an "a-ha" moment. After years of disrupting and heralding change in organizations, I had created a model for what I was doing. A technique for identifying the way people approached change and collaborated (or didn't) with others. It turns out that disruption is only a small part of it, and the magic is in the balance.

It's easy to put people into two categories: one for the supporters and one for the naysayers. And for many years, I did that. However, some naysayers can easily be convinced, while some supporters are like vapors. Our brain loves to bucket things. But bucketing people, especially in such a binary way, is fraught with disappointment.

I have always seen patterns in people. Some were like me, ready and willing to take disruption on. Others seemed to adjust, quickly looking for ways to optimize or create efficiencies for the upcoming change. Still, others dug their heels in, questioned everything, and insisted on all the answers, in detail, right away.

The Sustainable Disruption Model (SDM) is a thought model that will help you understand why you approach change (and the disruption that often goes along with it) the way you do. This isn't necessarily about how companies can be better about disruption. This was written to help people understand. Because people are at the heart of any disruption, people lead it, stop it, build it, improve it, harness it, or ignore it. As we all consider what AI brings to our organizations, the ability to empower people to lead through this disruption will be an important differentiator.

Balance is the key to lots of things, and that's true for disruption. The reason I make a terrible employee is because I have a difficult time being satisfied. When something is well-established and ready to manage, I get bored. I crave the chaos of blowing stuff up. The good news is there are other types of people, too: Optimizers and Keepers. We will explore each of these profiles and better understand the peaks and valleys of each, along with the tendencies they often identify with.

Disrupters are comfortable with change. As a matter of fact, they often court change. Disrupters are driven to unsettle the norm, challenge conventions, and ask questions others won't. Disrupters need to experiment, which means they are great at building things from scratch but not so great at managing the status quo. They approach problems in a novel way. AI is like a siren's call for most Disrupters. Not only is it new and exciting, but it also promises to bring significant shifts to almost every aspect of our daily lives.

Optimizers are driven by improvement. They want to see all things made better. Some Optimizers are driven by scale, but scale and improvement are often the same. Optimizers light up when given the challenge to operationalize a fledging idea. They take what's already there and keep improving it. They tweak it until it runs smoothly. Optimizers think a lot like Disrupters but with one small caveat: they don't always like to blow stuff up and start from scratch. They'd rather see what they can make out of what exists. Optimizers' relationship with AI will help organizations ensure that they create efficiencies. The more Optimizers, the less likely you will scale chaos.

Keepers are called that because they excel at keeping the lights on, the doors open, and the paychecks coming. Keepers are essential to an organization's ability to sustain itself. They are the eye of the storm often brought on by Disrupters. They will do what it takes to keep things the status quo. For Keepers, AI is terrifying. We have to respect that the reaction isn't because they're "old-fashioned" or refuse to change, but rather because repeatability and consistency are their superfoods. AI will disrupt all that for Keepers, and for Keepers and the organizations they live in, that means upheavals galore.

For clarity, I want to posit several definitions. Definitions that make important distinctions about what it takes to disrupt. Let's first delineate between disruption and disruptive. Disruptive is behavior, and disruption is the experience of said behavior. One more important nuance is that there's a difference between a Disrupter and someone being disruptive. It's an important nuance that we see all the time. Anyone can be disruptive. It does not mean they are, as we will define later, Disrupters.

An easy way to think about this is the difference between Steve Jobs and Elon Musk. Steve Jobs was a Disrupter. He was monomaniacal. He had one pursuit and that was Apple. He was purposeful in his disruption, starting with the personal computer and expanding from there. But the intent was always to build Apple by blowing up whatever convention held back the way you think about interacting with technology. For most of us today, we can't imagine a different way. Our day-to-day experiences now are indelibly marked by Steve Jobs's obsessions. A true Disrupter.

This will be a controversial position, but I believe Musk is disruptive, not a Disrupter. By the way, it is not a bad thing to be comfortable with disruption—it's just different from being a Disrupter. Musk is a living embodiment of a disruptive mentality. His financial security allows him to amplify those areas that he sees as opportunities. He's good at identifying opportunities, but I don't believe disruption to be his primary objective. From Tesla to SpaceX to Twitter, he grows something that's already started. Each of these examples was disruptive, and Musk just jumped on the bandwagon with his money in tow. History is filled with people who used their comfort with disruption to step into a space that someone else started. But make no mistake, being comfortable with disruption and using your privilege to amplify someone else's work does not make one a Disrupter.

I also want to be clear that change is not the same as disruption. Change is constant, as we will learn in these pages. But disruption is (sometimes) the precipitating event. The "bang" that sparks a thousand subsequent "pows." We have recently lived through this exact scenario when ChatGPT went live in November 2022. There is a distinct "before" and "after." The waves of change had lulled us. We know the "pows" are coming. How can we better prepare for them? Therefore, when I talk about creating sustainable disruption, it is to help people (and sometimes companies) become better at smoothing out the sharp edges of disruption.

Every organization wants to disrupt before being disrupted. Yet it seems that organizations and industries are often surprised when everything they hold dear explodes to smithereens out of nowhere. From technology that shapes our lives to viruses that force us to reconsider how we interact—disruption comes from many different places. Can we harness disruption? Is it possible to take the good with the bad and purposefully change our world?

"There is nothing permanent except change."
(Greek philosopher Heraclitus)

Change is perhaps the only consistent thing we are talking about here. Its scale and impact may waver, but it is always there, strumming along. I've seen enough changes in organizations to know how most of it goes. I know the impact it has on people who are brought along for the ride. I can't be there to help everyone navigate through it. But if this sustainable disruption model helps one person, then the ripple of change will have started. So, let's get into it.

Something from Nothing

When I started this work on disruption, long before I started writing this chapter, I wasn't sure what to call it. Part of the challenge in those early days was that I wasn't sure what "it" even was, let alone how I would use it. Researching and learning new concepts to better understand is a normal part of my life and work. I had never attempted to turn previous concepts into *something*. Whatever that "something" would be. Before we get too far into the content, I want to address the "why me" question. Maybe you're not asking that, but I did. Why is a data consultant weighing in on disruption? While doing research, I noted that most of the books I read that covered this topic were written by people with a big education from fancy schools. Many had a background in management consulting or executive coaching. I had a big case of imposter syndrome. My personal affinity for disruption aside, seriously, who do I think I am?

Here's how I answered that. I have spent my entire career on the cusp of one of the biggest, most disruptive, staggering changes that have happened to business since the Industrial Revolution. Data. Now, data has heralded yet another disruptive change: AI. I've seen disruption and change *from the inside*. I've been on the front lines, selling the "change" that data brought. Helping people navigate challenging situations for their own personal reasons. I've seen companies thrive and grow and other companies crash and burn. It doesn't have to be that way. Everything you need to navigate the disruptive change that AI heralds is already there. In your team.

What is a Thought Model?

Each time I spoke to people about my work on disruption, I asked how they would describe it. A theory seemed the most obvious way to describe what I was doing, particularly since there is no empirical data behind it, only years of anecdotal observation. Most of those years were through the lens of a consultant or leader in data and, therefore, had a specific frame. As I observed people, I discussed these concepts of disruption. So, the anecdotal data was skewed because, as we know, the nature of observing changes its behavior. This is where I tend to get into trouble because I want all the data. All the research. All the things must coalesce into a wave of unimpeachable quality. That is not this work. I spent several months in that place, unable to describe it. I didn't stop working on it, though. Then I read Carlota Perez's "Technological Revolutions and Financial Capital: The Dynamics of Bubbles and Golden Ages." I picked it up because I was convinced that innovation was cyclical. Macro and micro cycles. If that were true, we could predict behaviors and their associated responses. Perez's book was a revelation.

Perez is a well-known and respected economist. Even in her introduction, she struggled to define exactly what her work represented. In her words, I found a reassurance but also a description that resonated. Perez says, "This book is a think-piece, the spelling out of an interpretation..." and refers to the narrative as a way of transmitting the "Thought Model." A thought model is a way to identify and change unintentional patterns. It is often used in therapy, but it's very applicable here. By its nature, a thought model is dynamic and oftentimes disruptive. Changes to thought models are part of the process. As behaviors change, patterns change. Ta-frickin-da! A thought model.

Sustainable Disruption Model

In the next section, I will detail each of the profiles of this disruption model. Here, I will describe the three profiles and explain how the model operates. I find it easiest to start with what it is not. It is not a continuum. Most people do not float back and forth between the three, suggestive of a continuum. The people who have been part of the testing for these profiles indicate a strong affinity toward one or sometimes two. This is how I determined that people could have a primary and a secondary that make up their profile. You may even find a scenario where someone sits in a different profile for a period of time because the situation demands it. For example, a Keeper being an Optimizer or a Disrupter being an Optimizer. It's not a natural state for them, and if forced to do that for too long, they will burn out.

Unlike things like the Myers Briggs model that claims that if you answer honestly, you are what you are regardless of time and circumstances. I believe these profiles to be dynamic. Circumstances that create stress, such as parenting or working so you can pay the bills, are sufficient to demand that we shift. Everyone has a primary, which is your preferred state. Most have a secondary, but all of us can be any of them for a short period of time, if needed. I considered the impact of age to be the precipitating factor. Young people are generally more comfortable with disruption. Especially the type that challenges societal expectations and standards. This is true because they have yet to experience the immense pressure that occurs to stay within the confines of what has been defined. Yes, they get some of that in school, but they also get the message to "be yourself" and to not let other people define you. Yet when you get into the "real world," you're not encouraged to be yourself. You're encouraged to toe the line. If you challenge too much, then the overwhelming pressure of staying put kicks in. If you push back and say, "f-ck the man" that means all those people before you were wrong. The high school popularity contest is barely a trial run. This is the big leagues, and I am here to tell you they play for keeps.

This is why you often see people being disruptive, and then, in the middle years, they soften their stance. Only to get arrested for protesting in their 60s (or beyond). It's because the pressure of the middle years to "stay in your lane" is too much, especially when raising kids, paying a mortgage, taking care of elderly parents, etc. This is where the rush to judgment in this anecdotal observation method can force you to draw potentially false conclusions. For example, maybe you take the quiz and think you're a Keeper, but your profile says you're an Optimizer. Then you realize that your life circumstances made Keeping much easier than Optimizing. Have you heard the phrase; actions speak louder than words? Your actions dictate which of these profiles are primary. When you have so much in your life that's already disruptive (like young children), disrupting at work is not as important. Your bucket is already full. When I talked with people, they placed themselves into one of the three of the profiles. They often say, "I've always been like that since I was a kid, I ...." Sometimes circumstances force us to adapt, to survive—it's what makes us human.

I settled on the term "Sustainable Disruption Model" because it is, at the heart, a thought model. Driven by circumstances, acted out in behavior, finding patterns, and then modifying them. I want to be clear: all three profiles make up sustainable disruption. While it is common for most of us to think that disruption is first or most important, the reality is that without the other two profiles, any disruptive idea, thought-model, innovation, or invention is a blip. And history is full of them.

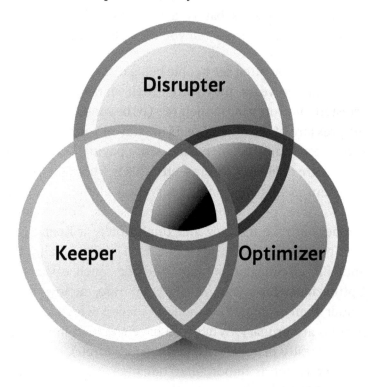

Figure 4.1: Venn Diagram of Disrupters, Optimizers, and Keepers.

Disrupters | Optimizers | Keepers Profiles

I'm proud of my Disrupter mentality if you haven't picked up on it yet. I tend to approach problems in a different way than a lot of people. It is what makes me a great consultant and a terrible employee. Over the years, companies have hired me to build something from scratch. For that work, disruption is a natural, powerful tool. But after finishing, it's time to manage it. Well, that's when things get boring for me and terrifying for everyone else.

A while back, I presented on how organizations can innovate in times of chaos and churn (you know, modern times) while not burning people out. Most organizations don't do this well, and many can't do it at all. The natural inclination when things get crazy is to buckle down and stay the course—unless you're a natural Disrupter like me. I'm like Lieutenant Dan in Forest Gump, strapped to the top of the crow's nest, egging the storm on. You need people like me. All organizations need someone who can *thoughtfully* disrupt. The real trick is how much.

Disrupters

> "On what poor, pitiful, defenseless planet has my monstrosity been unleashed?"
> Jumba from Lilo & Stitch

Much has been written about Disrupters. When I started this work, I thought this content was about Disrupters. As a matter of fact, an early title of a book was "A love letter to Disrupters." But the more I read and researched, the more I realized that Disrupters get all the love (and hate, too, but that's always the way it is). This is particularly true when you look at books written for a business audience. It is as if all Disrupters are alchemists. Because they exist in your organization, they will transform your profit margin or extend your product line. I have lived in corporate America for most of my career, and while those books put Disrupters on a pedestal, most organizations do not. As a matter of fact, most organizations in their day-to-day would rather never have a Disrupter because we challenge everything and ask hard questions.

The status quo "that's the way we've always done it" mentality is precious to most organizations. It creates a sense of calm and order. Many stories exist about organizations that kept that sense of order right into bankruptcy court. From Kodak to Blockbuster. In both cases, they had Disrupters warning them to no avail. We can all look at that in hindsight and cast judgment. But the truth is that if your industry was on the cusp of a true disruption, you probably wouldn't be much different.

Part of the challenge is that Disrupters are human. Sometimes, we are tactless, poor communicators or introverts, often too low in the organizational hierarchy to send warning signals to the right person. When interviewing people who were self-proclaimed Disrupters, I found a big variation from "alpha" Disrupters who love to blow stuff up to see what happens to slow followers who disrupt but are often prompted by thoughtful consideration.

> *"The culture at large companies is typically built on a foundation of operational excellence and predictable growth. Change-makers trying to conduct experiments are rarely greeted with open arms — especially when they're working on an idea that may cannibalize stable businesses or upend today's distribution model."[32]*

Many Disrupters were driven by a cause. I interviewed a "mama bear" who challenged her school district's lack of support for kids with ADD. Sometimes, a Disrupter is an Optimizer with disruptive tendencies who just ask themselves, "If I don't, who will?" For example, a woman saw big discrepancies in pay and equity in a new job and called it out, heralding an organizational change that left several people unemployed. Some voluntary, some not.

Distinctions are important, especially when we start to think about who fits each of these profiles. You can disrupt without being a *Disrupter*. Being a megalomaniac and being egged on to do something disruptive is not the same as carrying a torch and burning stuff down because it's wrong. But admittedly, there is a fine line.

Challenging the status quo is an act, not a slogan. Doing disruptive work can hurt people's feelings. It can create

---

[32] https://hbr.org/2018/07/the-biggest-obstacles-to-innovation-in-large-companies?utm_medium=social&utm_campaign=hbr&utm_source=LinkedIn&tpcc=orgsocial_edit.

churn and chaos. Disrupters without Optimizers and Keepers mean nothing productive comes from the pain. That's as true in your personal life as it is in your corporate life. As we have seen, those companies that hold on too tight are exactly the ones that fail. Every organization would rather disrupt than be disrupted. You should court disruption because the harder you fight it, the more likely it will win. What has always been missing isn't the Disrupters, it's the Optimizers and Keepers.

In each section, after the description of the profiles, there are a set of questions. These questions are true and false. The more you answer "true" or "yes" to a question, the more you will identify with that profile. Answer all the questions. The profile for which you have the most affirmative answers is your primary, your preferred state. The next most is your secondary, or your tendency, which operates more like an inclination than a preference. This is not a static thing. If you're surprised by the results, consider your current situation. Are there circumstances in your life that are forcing you to adapt? If you know you're more of an Optimizer than the responses show, you may very well be adapting your perspective to meet your situation.

Disrupter Profile Questions

1. I like my day-to-day to be filled with variety.

2. If I see something that needs changing, I don't hesitate to instigate the change.

3. I like roles where I have a lot of autonomy.

4. I have been called a "rebel."

5. I crave change. Whether it's from shifting tides in the strategy to organizational structure changes. Even new methods or processes. Change helps me stay engaged.

6. Organizational change gets me excited for the future.

7. I get bored easily.

8. Rules and policies irritate me.

9. I like "greenfield" opportunities where I can create what I think is best.

10. I don't enjoy documenting.

11. I dislike maintenance tasks.

12. I like to create the "art of the possible" vision statements.

Optimizers

"Let's organize this thing and take all the fun out of it."
A cartoon that was taped to the cabinet in the Psychology Department at UW-Stout during my time there.

Several years ago, in an attempt to "relax," I booked a spa weekend with a friend of mine, let's call her Quinn. It was supposed to be a weekend to refresh and recharge. To commune with nature, eat well, and exercise. It was the spring after I released my first book. I was a traveling consultant and a mom of a (very) precocious five-year-old. I was exhausted, in more ways than one.

The pictures of this spa showed expansive rooms, a pond with walking trails, incredible food, and comfortable accommodations. We arrived late on Friday to what can only be described as a disheveled compound. If it wasn't for the sign in the front yard announcing we had arrived in the right spot, I would have assumed we were pulling into someone's home. Walking into what should have been a reception area, it was dark and not welcoming. It was out of date and smelled old, as if the windows hadn't been opened since a Flock of Seagulls had run away. We each went to our individual accommodations. Hers in the "barn," a new space for those who wanted the ability to stretch out. My room was in the house, upstairs, the third door on the left. It had a chenille bedspread, just like my grandmothers in her guest room. The fireplace was non-operational and foreboding, serving to weigh down the room. The bathroom was a shrine to avocado tiles. It had two showers. One bathroom but two showers? One was a bath/tub combination. The other was a walk-in shower shoved behind the door. You had to close the door to open the shower door. The view was the one bright spot (pun intended). It was spectacular: you could see the grounds with a large pond, trails, and gardens.

As Quinn and I wondered if we had made a mistake and plotted our escape, she asked me, "If you owned this place, what would you do?" I joked and said something like light a match and collect the insurance. Then she responded with, "I can't help but think there's something amazing here. If you just..." and then proceeded for the next couple of hours to describe every change she would make to improve the place. We walked the grounds, and she continued her renovation. Her enthusiasm was so palpable I got wrapped up in all the excitement. I offered some helpful ideas, like food that didn't make you want to go foraging in the forest for protein.

Quinn is an Optimizer. Her job was always in operations. She is great at taking ideas, new or old, and polishing them until they shine.

Optimizer Profile Questions

1. Inefficiency bothers me.

2. I'm comfortable navigating change for a good cause.

3. I enjoy the process of making something better (or improving something).

4. I can easily spot areas for innovation.

5. I like to push the status quo.

6. I often have ideas for product or service extensions.

7. I enjoy working with like-minded people.

8. I enjoy facilitating sessions that bring contrary groups or ideas together.

9. I often think about building for scale.

10. I'm better at reacting to content than creating it on my own.

11. I seek out roles that allow me to innovate.

12. I don't need a roadmap to follow. I can create my own.

Keepers

> *"Those who tell the stories rule the world."*
> *Native American Proverb*

I know a lot of Keepers because "data" attracts them. I use the quotes to be specific here, I mean the data that is binary. Not the information that is the end result of collating data. Data never lies, it's consistent, it has natural boundaries, and it excels when there are standards. Each Keeper has challenged me in different ways. One of the truisms about this thought model is that Keepers and Disrupters often live in very different head spaces.

A shining example of a Keeper is someone I will call Daisy. Daisy and I worked together. Because we were in corporate America, and they love their hierarchies, I was her leader. This is important because, as a result of the nature of our relationship, Daisy deferred to me. She did that because she follows rules, because she's a Keeper, which was hard because, as a Keeper, she wanted to follow my decisions. But as a Disrupter, I was shaking her foundation left and right. It was traumatic for her, and in my Disrupter ways, I didn't really care. I saw it, don't get me wrong. But I was there to do a job that required a lot of new ideas and ways of doing things. Caring about how someone was feeling was not first on my list.

Eventually, Daisy started pushing back. Which I usually love, but in this case, it was grating. She pushed back because she needed consistency. She needed standards and specific ways of doing things. I needed the team to be nimble, adjust quickly, and be ready for anything. Daisy dug in, and she brought others with her. She thought I was wrong and crazy and decided that it was incumbent upon her to ensure something was left sacred. Ignoring these shifts and pushing the team harder created an "us versus them" dynamic on the team. All productive work stopped, and we became a heart that couldn't efficiently pump anymore.

If I had known then what I know now, I would have focused on bringing in more Optimizers (we had one, the poor thing). I would have found ways to keep something stable and consistent. I didn't need to blow up everything. That was just my preference.

Daisy and I found common ground by recognizing each other's strengths and acknowledging that we had to work to see eye to eye. I consider this experience one of the most important in my career. If it wasn't for Daisy, I would not be writing this book.

Keeper Profile Questions

1. I enjoy writing policies, procedures, or instructions for others to follow.

2. I regularly use checklists to keep up with tasks.

3. I get a great sense of accomplishment from everyday tasks.

4. My friends would describe me as steadfast or resolute.

5. I like my day filled with consistency.

6. I like being *the* expert.

7. There is only one right way to do things.

8. Organizational change (such as reporting relationship changes) makes me uncomfortable.

9. I am often the last person to adopt a change.

10. I like well-established roles.

11. I think innovation and disruption are over-rated.

12. Well-documented processes are important for success.

Without Optimizers and Keepers, no organization can innovate well. Yet, Disrupters like me get all the attention during times of big change. There would be no Walt Disney Companies without Roy. There would be no Apple without Woz. I'm saying Disrupters need others to help make their crazy ideas a reality. They need Quinn's and Daisy's.

What mix of Disrupters, Optimizers, and Keepers do you have on your team? I bet you can name those Disrupters almost immediately, as well as the Keepers. Too many Disrupters and chaos reign supreme. Too many Keepers and you will fail to keep pace with the modern world. Nothing but Optimizers and you'll forever be fiddling with things. You will never reach a steady state (particularly challenging in a product mindset).

Asking a Keeper (for example) to push their boundaries of comfort is the kind of stuff that leads to burnout. Asking a Disrupter to sit still and manage something will probably lead to them leaving. But not before they cause a little drama.

Some roles are a natural fit for their type. I don't know a lot of Disrupter CFOs, for example. Don't ask a Keeper to lead a start-up in a volatile industry like cryptocurrency (for what I hope now are obvious reasons). This is not a perfect science. It's not a science at all. Most people are too nuanced to be put squarely in boxes their whole lives. Some are capable of impressive feats of adaptation.

How to use SDM

After you answer all the questions and determine your primary profile, you can decide if you have a secondary one. For example, I'm very much a Disrupter, but I have several optimizing tendencies. Enough that, given certain circumstances, I may operate that way.

Now that you have the language for your individual profile, you can look to your team. How many people on your team fall into each profile? Do you have a lot of one type?

Depending on what your team does, the team profile needs to be balanced.

You need to strike a balance between their functional roles in your organization and their SDM profiles. For purposes of generalities, most organizations have three different types of functions: governance, management, and some version of innovation. The innovation group is highly dependent on your organization and what they see as innovation. It could be your product team or a task force; however it functions, it should be Disrupter heavy. On the other hand, the governance team should not be Disrupter heavy. The most you should have in there is someone with a mixed Disrupter profile, like an Optimizer with Disrupter tendencies. Since this book is about bringing AI into your organization, think about the makeup of your AI team (if you have one). Perhaps they're managing several functions of AI and are responsible for the day-to-day. If that's the case their SDM profiles will be a mixed bag.

Just like their profiles indicate, if you need to shake things up, make sure you have Disrupters on your team. If you need to create operational efficiencies, hire Optimizers. If it is time to set it and forget it, keep those Keepers.

	DISRUPTER	OPTIMIZER	KEEPER
DISRUPTER	D/D	D/O	D/K
OPTIMIZER	O/D	O/O	O/K
KEEPER	K/D	K/O	K/K

Figure 4.2: The SDM Profile Table.

A Moment for Keepers

Disrupters get all the praise. Optimizers win awards and get promotions. Keepers get none of these. Our society doesn't celebrate Keepers like the other two profiles because it's not as exciting. I remember seeing an advertisement in an airport several years ago. Something like "'That's how we've always done it,' the worst words any leader can hear" or something akin to that. I loved the sentiment. Because of my Disrupter mentality, the phrase, "That's how we've always done it," hit like a punch to the gut. I wanted to shake the person and point to how much easier or simpler life would be if they stopped doing the minimum. Boy, was I wrong.

If you think of "Keepers" as storykeepers, that's a good start. For most of the history of humanity, telling stories was an important, even lauded, role of any culture. It was the only way to ensure that people were remembered and traditions upheld. Perhaps the most important part of storytelling was to ensure that difficult lessons were not forgotten. As we all move forward into our brave new world, the role of storykeeping doesn't dissipate. It doesn't go away because something new and shiny is on the horizon (like AI). If anything, the role of these Keepers becomes more critical as we find a way to accommodate the new into the old.

When someone says, "That's how we've always done it," they tell you hard lessons were learned to get to where you are today. Every organization has an evolution in its processes and structures, and Keepers are the protectors of that. In their minds, on the other side, is nothing but chaos. I'm not saying that everything Keepers protect is sacred. I'm saying that the role of Keepers is critical to the future-ready we're building. Dismissing them as difficult or "old-fashioned" creates a vacuum. Without Keepers, we will forget that the only way to scale is to create consistency and repeatability. The building blocks of a solid foundation from which to launch. Those Keepers keep the lights on and the doors open. When they share the stories that got us here, they show us how not to lose our way.

If you're a Disrupter, you need a Keeper or two to keep you honest. Don't run away from what they are telling you. Listen carefully. Only then can you truly build sustainable disruption.

Five

All that Glitters (is not Disruption)

Now that we understand the three profiles, I need to present some information about disruption. Similar to understanding AI, understanding disruption will help us determine what we should do. There are so many misunderstandings about disruption. From generational impacts to myths. From your experiences with leadership to your personal perspective. Disruption is as much a living, breathing, dynamic entity as anything else we will experience. It is not just about AI or even technology. Disruption is humanity. Humanity is disruption.

Generations Speak

My dad turned 90 last year. He was born in 1933, and when I look at the pictures from his boyhood days, the few that remain, the shock of the generational impact is evidenced by those shadowy black-and-white images. Like many of his contemporaries, my dad lived through radically shifting times. We forget that because there aren't as many storytellers (or *Keepers* in our new parlance) around to share their lived experiences. And, as it does with most things, time has softened the edges of the pain.

He lived through a pandemic without the "benefit" of social media to give them up to the second updates on some stranger's experiences. He lived through several wars, one of which he experienced from the bow of a ship. He lived through the transition from horse to car, radio to TV, phone to cellphone to smartphone (which he hates, BTW). From no indoor plumbing to today's common conveniences. He thought the internet would save mankind. He is part of the "Silent Generation" from 1925 to 1944. According to Wikipedia, unlike the previous generation that fought the system, the silent generation was about working within the system. Generationally, they seemed much more likely to play it safe than take big risks.

I firmly believe that if you don't understand history, you're doomed to repeat it. When I started looking at the disruptive technologies that have changed my life (GenX) and noted the ones that changed my dad's life, the broader cycle of generational impact became obvious.

There's a phenomenon in which you think you're the only one. It seems we have that challenge generationally as well. Undoubtedly, the pace of change has increased dramatically within the last generation, which is a different issue altogether. Every generation has faced challenges that, at the time, felt transformative, but not always in a good way.

The television feels archaic now. The idea of programming that has specific times, laughable. Yet those grainy black-and-white images rocketed the baby boomers into the technological age. Families gathered for programming. Commercials were just as entertaining as the content they tuned in for. News shows were late to the programming game and only lasted fifteen minutes. Not every grisly thing that happened in the city was reported. Not until the assassination of Kennedy, when the entire nation watched transfixed as Lee Harvey Oswald was murdered on live TV. The nation watched a family grapple with a loss too great to bear, a personal loss of a father and a husband that was public for all to see.

Why do I bring up the generations? As generations cycle through, they bring with them the particular set of values that they teach their children. Then those children live through a certain set of experiences, and it creates its own values and so on. Disruption is a generational value, as we found in the difference between the silent generation and the one before it. Between Gen-Xers who have taken disruption as our mantra to subsequent generations who haven't felt as strongly about it (such as Gen-Z who are noted as being "risk-averse").

Pew Research[33] has been categorizing generations for over thirty years. They note that part of their algorithm is a shift in values and thinking, not long after the assassination of Kennedy, and Dr. Martin Luther King Jr, then Bobby Kennedy, a palpable shift occurred in the generations. It was no longer the post-war boom where you could have the American dream if you worked hard enough. It seemed as if the dream was over. Uncertainty, anger, and violence took over. Sounds kind of familiar, doesn't it? The values of the previous generations have their way of seeping through. While I am a GenX, both of my parents were born in the "Silent Generation," whereas my husband's parents are split; his mom is a late "silent generation," and his dad is a baby boomer. I can tell you that the differences between our upbringings are vast, and not just because I grew up in the country and he grew up in the city. Lessons and stories seep between and inform the next generation. Some stories get lost, and often, the hardest lessons have to be repeated.

When we talk about individuals and their comfort and willingness to be disruptive, we have to consider that some of that comfort may come from their environment and lived experiences. While researching, I met and interviewed people from all generations who claimed degrees of interest in disruption. In many cases, it is divergent from what one would assume their generation would support. After all, categories are broad concepts, not individual profiles. So, while the generation you grow up in

---

[33] https://www.pewresearch.org/short-reads/2023/05/22/how-pew-research-center-will-report-on-generations-moving-forward/.

may very well inform your perspective, it may not directly affect whether or not you embrace disruption.

That said, the question was raised as to the role of "Keepers" and whether or not this type would endure the generations when so much change was and is coming. It's important to understand that Keepers are rule followers. They like order, documentation, and processes. When you consider the generations of Millennials and beyond, it's natural to question whether those generations will harbor any keeping mentality. The answer is yes, they will. Any of these traits are inherent to an individual. While some generational impact may broaden their perspective to give a Keeper some Optimizer tendency, for example, it will not eliminate the Keeper mentality completely, which is a good thing for us.

Generations, according to Pew Research:[34]

Generation	Range
Silent Generation	1928- 1945
Baby Boomers	1946 -1964
Gen X	1965 – 1980
Millennials	1981- 1996
Gen Z	1997- 2012[35]

[34] https://www.pewresearch.org/religion/chart/generations/.

[35] https://www.pewresearch.org/short-reads/2019/01/17/where-millennials-end-and-generation-z-begins/.

Technology and Pace of Change

"Buckle up, buttercup" is the line that keeps going through my head. Yesterday, my sister sent me a picture of me getting my first computer. It was Christmas, and I only knew that because I was wearing a Christmas tree pin. My parents saved up to get me that clunky thing. I was already in college, circa 1994. Before that, I went to the lab to type up papers. This was before the internet was pervasive. I still went to the library to get onto the internet, for a while anyway. I got my first email in my last year of graduate school, 1998. Certainly, email existed before that, but there was no reason to get one. People still called up on a phone that sat, unhelpfully, I might add, at home chained to the wall.

The revolution wasn't televised.[36] It was brought to you on your phone because there's an app for that. Cellphones were everywhere when I had my first real job in Minneapolis. By 2003, I no longer had a "landline," and I've never looked back, all in the span of less than ten years. "Buckle up," indeed.

The same goes for my industry. When I started, we used software, but emailing reports was still impossible because the files were often too large. You printed the dumb things and put them in an inter-office envelope. Collecting data was easy because there wasn't much of it, at least not by comparison. I remember having data tables with thousands

---

[36] https://en.wikipedia.org/wiki/The_Revolution_Will_Not_Be_Televised.

of rows, which I thought was amazing. Data revolutionized the way everyone works. In the twenty-plus years that I've been at this, I've been on a rollercoaster ride. When I started, no one talked about data, and those of us who were responsible for it were considered "geeks." Now, everyone talks about data, from the likes they get on their posts to the news it makes every day. Data, data everywhere.

As I started this project, I fully expected to find people who were more disruptive than me and who I knew would change the world. I was naïve to think that technology wouldn't disrupt me. It's been a long time coming, from AI art to automated content creation for social media—it was just a matter of time. My Disrupter mindset kicked in quickly for me, though. I found ChatGPT unsettling but soon realized the potential power. Since I had written so much content on data governance, I reached out to Tom Niccum to explore creating a personalized Chatbot. The experience helped reassure me that, yes, the technology was cool, but we're still a bit away from a bot taking over my job.

My work on disruption has always been dedicated to the people. The ones that disrupt, optimize, and keep, and this work is meant to highlight ways to embrace each other and the different gifts we offer. But what do we do when technology does it? Especially when you're fully unprepared for the impact. The reality is you're never prepared. It's a bit like parenting, you can read books and talk to friends, but nothing will prepare you for the experience.

ChatGPT grew to 100 million users in 2023, within one year after being released. It took cell phones 16 years to reach the same milestone.[37] Amazon Kindle has over 500 books "co-authored" by ChatGPT. I used the quotations around co-authored because any claim of "authorship" by ChatGPT is a stretch to me. With that said, I've decided to let ChatGPT[38] write this section on the role of technology in disruption. The content below was written by the bot and edited (where needed) by me.

Me: What is the role of technology in disruption?

ChatGPT: Technology plays a crucial role in disruption across various industries and sectors. Disruption refers to the significant and often transformative changes that alter the way businesses operate, deliver products or services, and interact with their customers. Here are several ways in which technology contributes to disruption:

Innovation and Creativity: *Technology facilitates innovation by providing tools and platforms that enable individuals and organizations to create new products, services, and business models. Disruptive technologies often emerge from innovative ideas that leverage technological advancements.*

Efficiency and Productivity: *Technological advancements improve efficiency and productivity in various processes. Automation, artificial intelligence, and machine learning, for example, can streamline operations, reduce costs, and*

---

[37] https://www.livemint.com/technology/tech-news/chatgpts-meteorical-rise-100-million-users-in-2-months-11677997670518.html.

[38] As of this writing I used ChatGPT3.5, newer versions were available for a fee.

increase overall productivity, enabling businesses to disrupt traditional models.

Access to Information: *The digital era has democratized access to information. This has empowered consumers and businesses with knowledge, enabling them to make informed decisions and challenging traditional structures. Disruption often occurs when new entrants leverage information to offer alternatives that meet the evolving needs of consumers.*

Digital Transformation: *Organizations that embrace digital transformation leverage technology to revamp their business processes, models, and customer experiences. This can lead to the displacement of established players by more agile and technologically savvy competitors.*

Platform Economics: *Technology platforms, such as social media, e-commerce, and sharing economy platforms, create new ways for businesses to connect with consumers and deliver services. These platforms can disrupt traditional industries by offering more efficient and user-friendly alternatives.*

Data Analytics: *The ability to collect, analyze, and derive insights from large datasets has become a powerful tool for disruption. Businesses can gain a competitive edge by leveraging data analytics to understand customer behavior, optimize operations, and identify new market opportunities.*

Blockchain and Decentralization: *Technologies like blockchain enable decentralization and disintermediation, reducing the reliance on central authorities. This has the* *potential to disrupt industries such as finance, where traditional intermediaries are replaced by decentralized and more transparent systems.*

Mobile Technology: *The widespread adoption of mobile devices has transformed how people access information and services. Disruption often occurs when businesses leverage mobile technology to offer more convenient and accessible solutions.*

Internet of Things (IoT): *IoT connects physical devices and enables them to communicate and share data. This can lead to disruptive changes in various industries, such as healthcare, manufacturing, and transportation, by improving efficiency and creating new opportunities.*

Rapid Technological Change: *The pace of technological change itself can be disruptive. Businesses that fail to adapt to new technologies risk becoming obsolete, while those that embrace change can gain a competitive advantage.*

In summary, technology is a key driver of disruption, enabling innovation, efficiency gains, and new ways of doing business. Embracing and adapting to technological advancements is essential for organizations to thrive in an ever-evolving landscape.

I noticed that it didn't reference AI as disruptive, so I asked this question.

Me: Is AI a disruptive technology?

ChatGPT: Yes, artificial intelligence (AI) is widely considered a disruptive technology. AI has the potential to significantly impact various industries and sectors by introducing new capabilities, enhancing efficiency, and transforming traditional business models. Here are several ways in which AI can be disruptive:

Automation: *AI technologies, such as machine learning and robotic process automation, can automate repetitive and mundane tasks. This not only increases efficiency but also allows organizations to allocate human resources to more strategic and creative endeavors.*

Data Analysis and Insights: *AI enables sophisticated data analysis and pattern recognition. Businesses can leverage AI to extract valuable insights from large datasets, helping them make data-driven decisions and gain a competitive edge.*

Personalization: *AI-powered algorithms can analyze user behavior and preferences to deliver personalized experiences. This is evident in sectors like e-commerce, entertainment, and marketing, where personalized recommendations enhance customer engagement and satisfaction.*

Natural Language Processing (NLP): *NLP allows machines to understand and respond to human language. This has led to the development of virtual assistants, chatbots, and other applications that improve customer service, automate communication, and streamline interactions.*

Healthcare Advancements: *AI is making significant contributions to healthcare through applications like diagnostic tools, predictive analytics, and personalized* *medicine. These innovations have the potential to improve patient outcomes and reduce healthcare costs.*

Autonomous Vehicles: AI is a key component of autonomous vehicle technology. The development of self-driving cars has the potential to disrupt the transportation industry, impacting not only traditional car manufacturers but also related sectors like insurance and logistics.

Financial Services: AI is transforming the financial industry by enhancing fraud detection, risk management, and customer service. Automated trading algorithms, robo-advisors, and AI-driven credit scoring are examples of disruptive changes in finance.

Creativity and Content Creation: AI can be used to generate content, including art, music, and writing. This has implications for creative industries and may challenge traditional notions of human-exclusive creativity.

Supply Chain Optimization: AI can optimize supply chain operations by predicting demand, improving inventory management, and enhancing logistics. This can lead to cost reductions and increased efficiency throughout the supply chain.

Security and Cybersecurity: AI plays a crucial role in cybersecurity by identifying and responding to security threats in real-time. It enhances the ability to detect and mitigate cyber-attacks, making it an essential tool in the evolving landscape of digital security.

The disruptive nature of AI arises from its ability to automate, analyze vast amounts of data, and perform tasks that were once exclusive to human intelligence. As AI continues to advance, its impact on various industries is likely to grow, leading to both challenges and opportunities for businesses and society as a whole.

Why ChatGPT didn't first include AI in its list is unclear.[39] It is not a perfect tool, but it's an interesting one and, in many ways, could help content creation (as it did here). As it evolves, the specificity will improve (such as by including AI in the list of disruptive technologies). Now, we are at the helm of a generation that can use ChatGPT for a whole host of things we never expected. It can answer any question you can imagine, but it is not always accurate. Of course, the risk is we start to rely too much on these tools to inform our worldviews because these are just a reflection of a subset of content, and that content can (and likely is) be skewed in some ways. For example, I asked, "Who writes about disrupting data governance?" I expected it would mention yours truly, since I published a book called "Disrupting Data Governance" in 2019. But ChatGPT didn't identify me in the list. Even ChatGPT is at the mercy of algorithms.

It's Not Just About Leadership

When I started this work, I had a few assumptions. The primary one that hung me up for a few years is that it was

---

[39] Considerable discussion occurred about this at Moxy World HQ. The point being, the question you ask, and the way you ask it, is very important.

only about the Disrupters. I felt that Disrupters and disruption had gotten a bad reputation, which, in hindsight, is ridiculous because all we ever hear about are the Disrupters. All we ever read about are the Disrupters, and oftentimes, those Disrupters are leaders. So much so that many people equate the ability to disrupt an industry with a compelling chief executive.

I've worked in corporate America for most of my career. As a result, I've had the privilege to work with and for lots of different types of people. I can tell you that in none of those experiences, regardless of the situation, were the Disrupter-CEOs the ones "getting the work done." They were directing the work and definitely influencing what got done when. But along that chain of command were several Optimizers and Keepers executing the vision.

For years, that was what was missing in the work on disruption. Yes, disruption and Disrupters are cool. They bring about so much change, some of which we like, but they are not the only ones doing it. It cannot only be about leadership. At the rate and pace of change that we are all experiencing now (it's not just AI), there is no way that one leader, no matter how charismatic and brilliant, could keep up. Just because you're a leader does not mean you are a Disrupter—many are Optimizers or Keepers.

Yet the focus has often been on the brilliant Disrupters that lead. Especially when that leadership looks traditional, like in a hierarchal organization with a title that has been bestowed upon them. To be in that rare air, you must fit a pre-determined mold, which can limit a creative, diverse way of thinking.

In our modern world, organizations need to be nimble. Large, top-down bureaucratic organizations are not that. The ability to pivot and adjust to shifting trends requires a degree of awareness. A willingness to let people lead from where they are, even if they are buried throughout your enterprise leading by influence (because a title was not bestowed upon them).

The Myths of Disruption

Recently, my business partner bestowed upon me the best title ever given to a person. I am the "Chief Blow-Sh*t-Up Officer" for Moxy Analytics. It is not just that I love challenging the status quo. It's important for us to think about what we do and how we do it.

Don't take it for granted because it's always been that way. Disruption is no different. So, let's break down the things we hear about disruption all the time and see which ones stand up to the test.

Myth Number One

It requires a brilliant alpha-Disrupter (usually male, often white) to show us the way.

This is a myth for a couple of reasons. The first is because this is what we often hear in media. Second, because not all Disrupters are alpha Disrupters, the trouble is that when they are, they tend to get a lot of attention. Let's look at one example (of several that exist).

I am not a big old movie buff. I find them stiff and slow. Until I learned about Hedy Lamarr.[40] Hedy Lamarr was born in Austria and was a film star during Hollywood's golden age. She emigrated to America during World War two and was racked with guilt about the family she left behind. She always loved math and technology and, by many accounts, was a genius. She invented the base technology of Bluetooth. An actress invented something that helps me take calls in my car or connects my iPhone to a speaker. Touted to be one of the most beautiful women of her time, she partnered with a musician, George Antheil, to create a communications system that guided torpedoes with more intention. The "frequency-hopping" that prevented torpedoes from being intercepted is what we now use daily. The patent and military uses didn't come to fruition in time to help the war effort. For a very long time, her partner, George Antheil, was given credit. But Hedy was the Disrupter, and an alpha one at that. She was just born the wrong gender and too pretty to be taken seriously.

Myth Number Two

All Disrupters are jerks.

Challenging the status quo is an act, not a slogan. But doing that work hurts people's feelings and creates churn and

---

[40] https://www.womenshistory.org/education-
resources/biographies/hedy-lamarr.

chaos. Disrupters tend to come across as tone deaf, at a minimum, and often narcissistic. From the story I told in the last chapter about Daisy to the long-standing stories of Steve Jobs and his monomaniacal behavior.

No one is a jerk 100% of the time. But doing the work of disruption requires tuning out the inevitable noise and staying on course. Steve Jobs is the most obvious example here. His obsession and youth created an environment that caused terror and stress for a lot of his staff. Another example is Elizabeth Holmes and her partner, Sunny Balwani. Both are now serving jailtime for their role in the fraud that took down Theranos. America's focus on alpha-Disrupters with crazy ideas caused many very smart people to get tricked. The idea was compelling. Elizabeth was smart, quirky, and conniving enough to get it to work. Stories abound about the work culture Ms. Holmes and Mr. Balwani built together. One wonders if they had built a culture based on mutual trust and respect. If they had allowed for the core idea to be the north star, would we all think about clinical lab tests differently today?

This is a strong myth because of these examples. Most Disrupters are getting the work done, not making headlines. For example, Marc Randolph, which leads me to my next myth.

Myth Number Three

Disrupters are lone wolves. They operate alone and do all the heavy lifting alone because they are that good.

No disruption happens alone. But often, we see the "Disrupter" praised and the work behind the scenes ignored. It doesn't make a story as compelling: "I had a great idea, and then several hundred people brought it to life through hard work and dedication." The click-bait era rather reads something like "Reed Hastings - Our Innovation Hero."[41] First and without a doubt, Reed Hastings is a Disrupter who has changed our world. We all love Netflix, and it has become part of our lexicon and spurred an entire industry. That's great, and he deserves credit, but he didn't do it alone. While doing research, I found a story about Netflix. Most of it talked about how amazing Reed was in the birth of Netflix. But it was the book "That Will Never Work" by Marc Randolph that opened my eyes. I recommend you read it. It's a great example of the team it took to get Netflix to become what we know today. It wasn't one guy with a brilliant idea, but Optimizers, Keepers, a couple of Disrupters, patience, and eventually, a corporate restructuring. It reads like a Daytime TV plotline.

Reed not only didn't do it alone, but he was only marginally involved in the beginning as the idea grew. I guess that story doesn't make for great headlines.

Myth Number Four

All disruption is good. (Or Bad).

---

[41] https://www.disruptorleague.com/blog/2011/12/04/reed-hastings-our-innovation-hero/.

Nothing is all good, or all bad. Often, time is the best deciding factor. The printing press was considered to be a terrible idea. Until it wasn't. Letting people pump their own gas prompted fear and outrage until, well, nothing happened. Video games were considered the devil's playground, and now it's normalized. AI will also suffer from this viewpoint.

Your perspective on whether disruption is good or bad is related to the disruption's impact on your day-to-day experiences. For example, while I consider myself quite disruptive, when ChatGPT came along, I only felt fear and resignation. I thought that it would replace me in my role as a writer about disruption. As we've seen, it can write but can't think like me. It can copy my words, but it can't distill down research and come to a novel conclusion. Not yet, anyway.

Myth Number Five

We're all lemmings to the disruptive leader. And it's all worth it.

The truth is that some of the best leaders are not Disrupters at all. They are Optimizers. I would consider Bob Iger[42] to be the best example of an Optimizer CEO. He understands the value of disruption. He has demonstrated his willingness to be disruptive. So, we can assume he's comfortable with it. But ultimately, he is very good at optimizing the mind-boggling number of touchpoints in a

---

[42] Check out his book, "Ride of a Lifetime."

corporation like Disney. He sees the importance of animation and unique content creation. He sees the value of the Disney experience and supports the operations of amusement parks. But perhaps most importantly, he sees how those two things work together in a way that few people can. He's a well-respected leader and can reconnect people in a way a "Disrupter" CEO would struggle with. We saw some of that as he reclaimed the helm at Disney after an abysmal performance by his successor.[43] Not all leaders are Disrupters with a pied-piper effect.

In our modern world, too few tools exist to help people understand their role in disruption. Most of them have been written for companies so they can survive and make more money. However, none of that would happen without the people who support that organization. The pace of change is a significant reason why I wrote this book now. I see the world and all its churn. I look back at how change, particularly technological advances, has only sped up in the last century. I know the pace of change will continue. I want to give people the tools and language to understand what that means for them. I want you to willingly leave an organization misaligned with your disruption profile because it's better for you. I want you to have a set of parameters and words that help you explain why you "dig in your heels" or "become a barrier" when changes come along.

---

[43] https://www.nytimes.com/2022/11/20/business/disney-robert-iger.html.

Teams and Maturity

When you bring people together into teams, it can be dynamic. Using SDM can bring another facet to life, particularly helpful when dealing with disruptions like AI.

There are a few considerations when you create teams with SDM in mind:

1. **Know your profile.** The secondary profile (i.e., are you an Optimizer with Disrupter tendencies) types will become handy.

2. **Seek balance!** Think of Optimizers (particularly primarily Optimizers) like a fulcrum. They balance everyone else out.

3. **What's your goal?** If you still think you need more Disrupters, but if you're already in deployment, Keepers are your best friends.

Keep in mind that the constitution of your team should shift as you move along a maturity curve (and maturity is not static, it changes over time). An average maturity model makes sense for our purposes, with one small modification. Most maturity models run from level one (chaotic), level two (repeatable), level three (defined), level four (managed), and level five (optimized). I am not interested in redesigning this because it's fine for what we need. I do have one small edit, and that is to flip levels two and three. I don't know how you repeat something that isn't defined.

Modified Maturity Model
Level One: Chaotic
Level Two: Defined
Level Three: Repeatable
Level Four: Managed
Level Five: Optimized

As you start this journey and ideate about AI, your teams should focus on Disrupters and Optimizers. I know a lot of organizations feel strongly that including more people is better. The reality is smaller teams move faster. If you want to achieve something as disruptive as AI, starting with a team full of Keepers will kill that fragile, innovative idea. This is where Keepers get a bad reputation. Brainstorming sessions lead them to tell you all the ways your idea won't work. They are processing barriers to see if they can identify them and work around them. All Disrupters hear is, "That will never work." Putting people where they can be the most successful is so important. It's also a terrible idea to put a Disrupter on a team once you have an idea and are ready to put it into production. That work is for Optimizers and Keepers. You can still be transparent, but don't hold the wrong people accountable.

But, like how?

The SDM is a tool in your ever-expanding toolbox. It is based on years of observation and work in the data space. I've talked to hundreds of people about it now. I've seen that as soon as I describe it, people start to use it in their lexicon. It makes sense. While it is not the end all be all, it gives us all a way to talk about disruptive work that helps *people* feel seen and heard.

When you start with the people, everything else follows. That's why most change management models focus on getting people to understand the change. Maybe they won't always be thrilled about it, but at least be okay with the change. The power of disruption isn't in technology. It's in the people. If people don't adapt, it won't work. Kodak knew about digital technology long before anyone else. Yet, the leaders of that organization refused to acknowledge it, spelling their doom. Blockbuster had an opportunity to acquire Netflix, but they thought it was an impossible business model, even after Netflix proved it worked. People make decisions every day about their role in disruption. See them and help them help you. Give them the words and tools to participate in your company's future in a way that respects the way they think and work. Then, nothing can stop you.

In the first part of this book, I talked about the need to be future-ready. Building platforms that assume obsolescence are built to pivot. What I'm proposing to you now, as we are about to bridge the gap between theory and practice, is that you can combine future-ready with the SDM to prepare for AI. These two things combine powerful data platforms that are ready for anything, with teams structured to take on disruption, not only at scale but with the ability to repeat it. Smooth out the edges of disruption so your organization can innovate from a place of purpose.

Six

Are You Ready for it?

In the first part of this book, we discovered the term "future-ready," and in the second part, we learned about the sustainable disruption model (SDM). In this last part of the book, we will bring the future-ready concepts together with SDM to create a framework. Governance is an important function for any organization taking on AI. I've spent the last five years working almost exclusively in governance functions. I have a lot to share. What it means to adopt responsible AI practices is related to the governance of AI. We will learn how the scale and speed of AI introduce a specific kind of risk to more vulnerable populations. Finally, I'm nothing if not pragmatic, and we will close out this book with a checklist. It's a long one, I won't lie.

Building a Mystery

Before we begin, if you still feel like AI is a mystery (and who doesn't?), consider a "special ops team." Somewhere in your organization (or network) are a few people who love to research and learn new things. There may even be a few that are good at teaching new concepts. Assign them the task to learn more about AI. Be specific and include different types, such as GenAI, or specific solutions like ChatGPT, RAG, or NER. Have them do lunch and learn brown-bag events. No one works for free, so keep that in mind. This way, you have empowered your team to upskill, and the organization benefits.

Based on what I've learned researching this book, here's how I would start a special ops team. First, I would have them do cursory research on AI's beginnings. It has a long history of more than seven decades. I would recommend they spend some time discussing and differentiating between the types of AI. All the hype has spurred a ton of confusion around AI and what's available today.

Clarity will be important as you start to think seriously about building capabilities. Finally, have them focus on the types of AI that might help your organization. Create a set of learning modules so everyone can take part. Make sure that you have a plan in place to evolve the content. None of this information will remain static (except the history of AI).

Plan for an on-going activity. Earlier we discussed the importance of data literacy[44] programs. Add an AI component to keep the learning coming. For the foreseeable future, technological changes and AI gains will change what's possible in your enterprise.

Culture Club

Building a sustainable model for disruption in your organization begs the question about your organizational culture. Working within the confines of how your organization thinks and acts will be an important part of your journey. While I talk about all these things being neutral, they are not. Introducing anything new can create consternation. One way to deal with this is to adopt a change management model.

Change management models are important when looking for ways to make critical shifts in your organization. When doing data work, change models are almost as important as the ubiquitous "people, process, technology."[45] For years in my consulting practice, I've added "culture" as the fourth pillar. Culture is a byproduct of people coming together in service of anything. People create a culture whether we

[44] https://www.dataleadershipcollaborative.com/data-practice/5-strategies-close-your-data-teams-ai-skills-gap.

[45] https://www.forbes.com/sites/forbestechcouncil/2022/12/29/is-the-60-year-old-people-process-technology-framework-still-useful/?sh=17d05bb04ab4.

realize it or not. People can change a culture, too. Here are a few models for intentionally implementing change management in your organization.

Several years ago, I learned about the "head, heart, hands"[46] model and liked its simplicity. It also has a great visual attached to it. I've tried using it, and while I think the average person understood it, I feel it is incomplete. It did come in handy, however, as a communication tool.

The most known change model is ADKAR[47] from Prosci. It stands for Awareness, Desire, Knowledge, Ability, and Reinforcement. It is probably the most well-established model in the change management space. It clarifies additional steps to take when leading change (beyond the head, heart, and hands). Several resources exist if you want to use ADKAR, from eBooks to classes. I've used ADKAR off and on for years.

Recently, a new change model came to my attention. It was built specifically for working in data by my friend Aakriti Agrawal. The ANCHOR[48] model stands for Aim, Need, Community, Hooray, Obstacles, and Resilience. I'm a little biased, but I think this model is brilliant. Primarily because it focuses on data, but also because it underscores the

---

[46] https://www.ncbi.nlm.nih.gov/pmc/articles/PMC9615563/.

[47] https://www.prosci.com/methodology/adkar#:~:text=
The%20word%20%E2%80%9CADKAR%E2%80%9D%20is%20an,of%20
more%20than%20700%20organizations.

[48] https://www.aakriti.dev/.

importance of having a specific aim, building community, and celebrating (hooray!).

But, First, the Elephant

The data industry has struggled for a long time to gain a seat at the table. Most organizations that have a CDO (Chief Data Officer) don't have them reporting to a CEO. The truth is that we, as an industry, have struggled to gain relevancy and trust. We're always discussing how to build trust and communicate or get the business to support our efforts. We are incredulous when they ask us for something and then "refuse" to help build it. We often use language like "they just don't understand" and spend too much time trying to deliver something to them. We can't explain why it takes so long to deliver what they asked for, and often, when we do deliver, we miss the mark. When there is a CDO, its tenure is often short, on average less than three years. Friends, we are on the struggle bus.

Then comes AI, with point solutions embedded in every piece of software you can buy. Now, ChatGPT can write code. Within the span of one year, our reason for being has been pulled out from under us. Now, thought leaders are saying that machines will determine data quality. There's a mad rush to take on AI projects as if being the last in that race ensures you're a fossil. If we don't disrupt ourselves, we won't have to wait too long for someone else to do it. It's on the horizon.

When I first started in the data industry, no one talked about people, teams, or organizational structure. We didn't discuss how to get the business to participate in our efforts. I don't ever remember discussing change management models. Maybe it was because I had a degree in psychology, but it was pretty obvious to me where the focus should be. It is so much easier to talk about the data, though, about the structure and systems of data. For too long, that was the focus of the data industry.

I remember working hard to create reports from business requirements only to discover that it wasn't what the business wanted. We struggled from day one to deliver because that was how we set it up. We created a separate team of "data" people with deep (sometimes obscure) technical knowledge. Then we told them they didn't need to talk to the business. Our data engineers, even our data modelers, didn't talk to the business. You'd think we all would have had business analysts who helped with that, but we didn't. Sometimes, we had analysts, or people like me, report writers. Bridge builders, that's what we were.

Before too long, the industry started seeing the need for more people to bridge the gap while still keeping those technical resources behind closed doors. While I lived through this example, many other organizations were experiencing (or continue to experience) something similar. We (the royal we, the "data industry") struggled that way for a while. Then something funny started to happen. We started to see the democratization of data. Tools started to add easy reporting solutions. People started to come out of school with some pretty deep technical knowledge, even for a business role. You would think the industry would have taken a collective step back, considered the current state, and made an important shift. But we didn't. Instead, we doubled down on the way we approached the work. That's when CDOs started to take hold. We thought the problem was that we didn't have an executive-level position. The problem all along was that we didn't embed ourselves into the business of our organizations. We are like Kodak. We knew what the problem was. We even invented the solution. We refused to make the needed changes to save ourselves.

So here we are. Now what? There are still bridges to cross, big ones. The thing that remains a challenge, even in our AI-crazed world, is the gap between business context and deliverables. Another way to think of it is domain knowledge versus functional knowledge. I talked to several people in the industry working to deliver AI-embedded point solutions. Every one of them said that we needed to find a way to focus more on the solution and less on the technology. More focus on the knowledge and less on the data. There is no doubt our industry will change, and the shift over the next five years will be significant.

How much of that shift will be our doing or done to us?

To solve this challenge, we have to think about what bridge we're actually building. Circa 2000, I moved to the Twin Cities to take a job as a "report consultant." The work was bridging IT and business at a big health insurance company. That was because the technical parts of data, architecture, modeling, engineering, and infrastructure all reported to IT. These functions were critical for us to deliver even the most basic report. We had to architect the data, model it, and then extract, transform, and load (ETL) it. Then, we used some pretty non-user-friendly systems to massage it into something useful. If we missed those first few steps, the query didn't return. And I can tell you that did happen, often. Then I'd call someone in IT, and we would talk it through until I could modify my query, or they would have to modify one step in their process. It required people like me to bridge that gap. Somewhere along the line, we stopped needing to bridge that gap.

Back then, 80% of the work to build a data repository was in the ETL. Moving the data from the source to the target. Our first sign was when the "technical" parts of data started to become less technical. Today, architecture, modeling, engineering, and infrastructure are either outsourced or glossed over. The super-computing power we have works out a lot of the kinks. Tech is becoming more democratized. As that happens, data teams are standing on a bridge to nowhere.

We still have a problem to solve. It's always been there. The only way AI will ever work is if we codify meaning and context. We have to do two things to create systems that mimic human cognition. First, we have to combine all types of data, structured and unstructured. Then, we have to do that in a way that provides context, not just meaning. You can define a word, but that doesn't give it context. AI has to codify everything, and that's both the problem and the answer.

The magic of data teams has always been in the ability to translate. We spent too long translating between business and IT. We should have been translating between meaning and context. We need to bridge the gap between narrow deliverables and broader business needs. The point solutions that we acquire, sometimes on purpose, are not so great. Over time, a lot of point solutions will create a Swiss chess effect, particularly for our business stakeholders, who will need to navigate between sophisticated AI functions and basic reporting across departments.

Disrupting Data Teams

I'm known for saying things others either won't say or don't say (outside of a conversation in the bar at a conference). Sometimes, my approach is way ahead of the curve. But other times, I hang out there saying what needs to be said. Here's another example. Get your data and analytics people out of IT. Put them all in the business departments.

They should focus on delivering solutions and knowledge, not technology. Quite honestly, it's been the problem for a long time. Asking data people to sit in IT and live with IT's problems while delivering relevant and timely data solutions to the business is very much like selling Taylor Swift tickets on Ticketmaster. Those technical issues are not the data team's problem. As these systems become more democratized, they will matter less and less anyway.

We see this shift in the broader IT teams for a while now. The cloud has been the tipping point for a lot of organizations. It's no longer about negotiating a server contract and figuring out how to stand that up. You don't need technical people to get them ready. It's all managed now through a Cloud Administrative Panel. Need more storage? There's a setting for that. We have commercialized the heck out of these systems. Cloud companies saw that the primary obstacle in organizations was people resources. There either weren't enough of them, or they didn't have the right skill set. They made these systems, from managing the cloud environment to creating sophisticated dashboards, as easy as possible. As business leaders started to pay for their own cloud instances, they wondered why a CIO was important at all.[49]

This isn't about an "us" and "them." It's about aligning where people work best and where they can deliver the most value to the organization. You may find that some folks in your data team think this is a terrible idea. They may be Keepers and they see the value in keeping the lessons learned nearer the technical platforms. Those calls will need to be made, but several things will have to change if you want to use AI in your organization.

One of the most important changes will be how your organization thinks about data. It is no longer a by-product of a system. It is ubiquitous. It oozes out from software, apps, and processes. It doesn't see organizational boundaries, nor does it see titles. You cannot control it. The best you can hope for is that you use it for good. Re-aligning teams to best take advantage of this "asset" (most of us don't treat it anywhere near an asset) is not only helpful, but it is also a responsible thing to do.

---

[49] https://www.cio.com/article/655183/the-cio-at-a-crossroads-evolve-or-become-a-dead-end-job.html.

The Re-org

People do the work, so we have to start here. The biggest impact will be moving your data and analytics people out of IT. To ensure that we make this shift, we have to ensure that the people doing the work are supported in the right way. Data is everywhere. It touches so much of our work lives. If someone in your organization spends 70% or more of their job on data and analytics, they should report to the CDO. If a person does 50-70% of their work in data, they should have a dotted-line relationship with the CDO team. Anything less than 50% and that person stays where they are at. One more little detail, the CDO reports to the CEO, always.

I've always thought about data teams as the front, back, and middle. I learned it working in restaurants where you have the "front of the house," the people interacting with customers. The "back of the house" is the kitchen staff (often not seen by customers). Then you have middle functions, bus people, or floor managers who go where they are needed. This structure stays pretty much the same for data teams. The only difference is the "back of the house" folks, the data architects, modelers, and engineers all report up through a business line now.

I can hear you grumbling from here. Some of you strongly feel that architects, modelers, and engineers are technical resources. Once upon a time, they were. They are not anymore. Leaving them in IT is doing us a disservice. It removes the architects, modelers, and engineers from the real work of understanding the context of the business that you're in. As we build our future-ready platforms, our job is to close the gap between the business context and the deliverables. We have to remove the artificial barriers between the technology of delivering accurate and timely data and business knowledge.

Any organizational restructuring is a change management challenge. This is no different. While you start to consider this change's impact, it's important to bring in your change management colleagues. Bring in a consultant if you don't have anyone in your organization that does change management. Every touchpoint in the organization will change. Muscle memory is difficult to overcome, but this change will create a foundation for the next wave of changes ushered in by AI.

Achilles Heel

While everything about our data programs must change, nothing changes. The existential threat isn't *just* from the models, the weighting, and tuning of parameters. It is the methods, standards, management, practice, and values that we use to create the data, manage the data, and build our teams. I know that most organizations struggle with fundamentals. These standard practices have now become paramount as we jump on the rocket ship that is AI. What do I mean? We have been so busy trying to meet the demands that we often gloss over critical steps. The politics of restructuring the teams can be a distraction. Just because we're moving the data team from IT doesn't mean we stop managing data. AI needs good data. I'll repeat that for those in the back: AI NEEDS GOOD DATA. We must focus on formally managing data across the lifecycle. We can re-org all we want. But, if we skip important stuff like managing the data quality, it doesn't matter where you sit in the organization. The data still won't be AI ready.

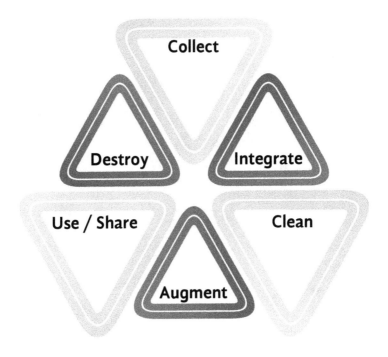

Figure 6.1: Data Management Lifecycle.

Theoretically, moving your data team will help align the work with the needs of the business. The business needs quality data. Helping them understand what that means and the work that goes into it will be a challenge. Just because we put these functions into the business doesn't mean they will understand and support it from day one. You will have some change management and a shared language to create.

*Don't lose sight of the need to manage the data.
All the things we were doing or supposed to be
doing when the team reported to IT are still there.*

Seven

Sustainable Disruption Model and a Framework for AI

F rameworks are great planning exercises, but they only work if you work them. If you're worried as you're reading this that it seems like a lot of work to set this up, then you're right, it is. The one true thing is that being thoughtful about what you're doing helps your organization stay on the right path. If you're unwilling to take some time to plan out what you're doing in AI, you have no business using AI. Remember, the speed at which AI allows you to scale is much higher than we've seen before. If you jump in without considering what comes after, you may start something you never intended. Take some time and plan it out. Having a touchstone is even more important when change is constant and disruption is volatile. Giving your organization something to check against reduces the volatility.

Most organizations start by buying point solutions with AI embedded in them. Sometimes, this happens when you didn't intend it to happen (I'm buying a piece of software, and it has "AI"). Sometimes, it's very purposeful (You must have "AI" in your software). Unless you have a ton of cash lying around or a company betting on AI, buying these point solutions is the easiest way to get started. In all honesty, most organizations cannot build AI capabilities. They lack the appropriate resources, money, or data. We will not address building AI capabilities from scratch. Instead, we will look at how any organization can start its AI journey.

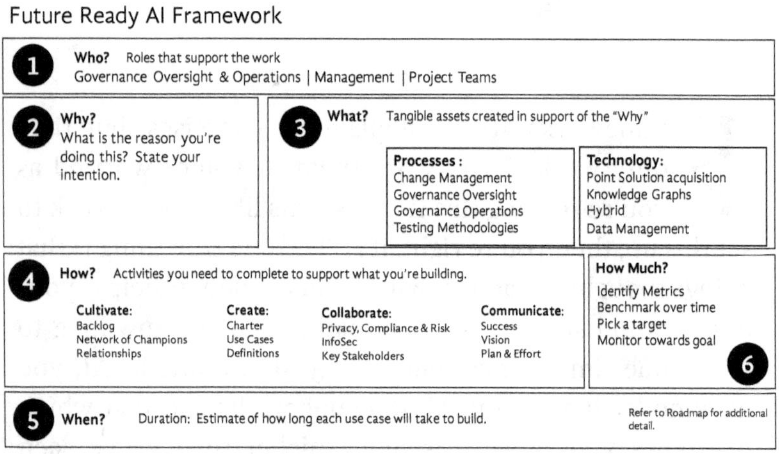

Future Ready AI Framework

Figure 7.1: Future-ready AI Framework.

We have to organize this work. One popular way is to create a framework. I like to think of frameworks as a "Strategy on a Page." It should cover the basics: who, what, when, why, how, and how much. Each section addresses a different aspect of your AI journey. In the figure above, I describe the intention in each box. The Appendix has a larger version with examples of what might go into each box.

Completing these frameworks prompts bigger questions about what work is behind each step. The framework doesn't have to answer all those questions but should provide enough information to inform an interested person. If the framework is a strategy on a page, then a playbook answers all the questions in detail. Together, we will learn about a framework for AI. You can then build your own playbook (see the Appendix for a sample table of contents for a playbook).

Who: Find Your People

In each step, the SDM team profile should look different. You don't want a Keeper trying to come up with new ideas all the time and you don't want a Disrupter trying to govern. Aligning towards strengths as you move through the lifecycle will allow you to move faster. Balance not only the SDM profiles but also the different types of knowledge. You will need business, operational, data, and technology knowledge and skills. Just because you don't want Keepers as part of the ideation phases doesn't mean you don't keep them up to date. Transparency is critical as you move as fast as you can through these phases.

Why: State Your Intention

This may seem a little "New Age," but stating your intention and the purpose behind what you're trying to do is a helpful step early on. It helps you to make decisions as you move along. If you're not sure what you're doing or why you're doing it, then it's much easier to get bowled over, sidetracked, or confused along the way.

Cover the basics. In the venerable words of Simon Sinek, know your "why." Are you doing this because you feel the pressure of competition? Because you're hoping it will build some efficiency? Because your CEO said so? Out of curiosity? Or you're a start-up whose entire business model is based on AI. Whatever the reason, know it, state it, and use it as your *foundation for all future decisions*. Change and disruption always happen. They feel more chaotic when you're being whipped about without a strong foundation. Your "Why," the reason you're attempting to do this at all, is that foundation. You need to know it and document it. Sharing it will be important, too, but we will cover that later.

Once you have your intention set, then ask yourself, "What if we're successful at _____?" While researching, I found a video of an interview with Shane Legg, cofounder of DeepMind. He shared (in a tone that felt too casual for me) that he had asked himself about the existential nature of AI. He admitted it might spell doom for our species[50] and

---

[50] https://www.youtube.com/watch?v=kMUdrUP-QCs&t=429s.

went forward anyway. Someone made the decision over and over again to continue creating a technology that could spell our doom. They thought, "Gosh, this could end humanity," and kept going. This question ("What if we're successful?"), is a smaller version of that. If you state your intention, such as "improving efficiency," then realize that if you're successful, more than 50% of your staff will not have jobs. Can you live with that? I'm not saying that there is a big moral judgment call every time, but sometimes there is. Getting in the habit of finishing the thought, "What if we're successful at _____?" can help determine the implications long before facing an existential crisis of your own.

What: Deciding what to Build

I circled around this for a very long time. I intended to provide pragmatic and salient advice because you can get the hype anywhere. I ran into trouble because there is not much out there in terms of specific guidance for the average organization. Yes, you can use some version of ChatGPT and fine tune the model to build a personalized bot. That hardly requires an entire book. At first, I wrote a bunch of stuff about technologies, but that felt disingenuous because the rest of the book is about people and solutions. But somewhere in this book must be the core of what to build. Nowhere else seemed as appropriate as the framework chapter.

The thing about frameworks is they are adaptable. I teach an entire class on building a data governance framework. Most of the class time explores what needs to be in the framework to best reflect the organization it serves. The "what" box of your framework could have different sections. Your "why" should inform your "what."

How: Methods to Collaborate, Cultivate, Create, and Communicate

This section should cover all the ways you intend to do the work. I include four areas when completing the "How" section. Collaborate, who do you need to work with? Cultivate, what things do you need to grow? To be successful, consider what's important to grow over time, such as a network of champions or relationships with key stakeholders. Create, what needs to be created and edited over time? Such as a charter or definitions. Finally, communicate a plan to ensure the organization sees what you're doing, from setting the vision to sharing the effort.

When: Setting Expectations

I promise you that when you start this, everyone will want to know what they will get and when they will get it. Set some reasonable expectations early on. It's best to leave the framework set to durations (such as two months). That ensures you don't have to worry about starting or ending at a specific time. The framework is meant to be a strategy on a page, not all detail. That said, part of the supporting documentation should be a fully planned out roadmap. Include start dates, end dates, and dependencies.

How Much: Metrics to Prove Value

We should all be thinking about how to prove that what we are doing works. Not all metrics are created equal. Of course, you can follow the SMART[51] method. But I'd encourage you to think about how long it will take to create a benchmark for the metric. Only then can you measure and finally set a target or goal. You will need time to benchmark the data to see where you land. Then, you will need to measure that benchmark over another period. That ensures you can track the rate of change over time. Only then should you pick a target.

---

[51] https://www.forbes.com/advisor/business/smart-goals/.

Variations on a Theme

All these steps are true regardless of your "why." Point solutions are everywhere now. Even for my small company, narrow bits of AI capabilities seem everywhere, from Chatbot customization to UI personalization on websites. It's hard to know what to do and when. The good news is that creating a framework helps create some guidance, something there is a shortage of when it comes to AI. In the spirit of guidance, I have a few more pieces of advice as you begin your framework.

People Power (Who Section)

Beyond the involvement of governance and executives, you must have some project teams of individual contributors that do the work. These smaller, more agile teams may come from all over the company. I like to call them the Future-Ready Agile Team (FRAT). Their SDM profiles should lean more towards Optimizers and Keepers. People will power this evolution. Not only do you have to balance the SDM profile, but you also need to balance top-down and bottom-up. That's the only way big changes are successful.

Identify Use Cases (How Section)

We have to start with some clear direction. Technology only solves well-defined problems. Work with your business peers to identify a few use cases with clear value.

Quantifying the value might take a little time, but do it now. It will help later when you're deciding what to build when. It will also help as you move through the steps.

Create a standard set of information that you gather for each use case. A title, description, current state problem, and how an AI project can fix it is a good start. Consider time to value (TTV) and some version of return on investment (ROI). Those things are related. The longer it takes to get to value, the less return you have. This is truer with point solutions and the hodge-podge approach than the knowledge graph. Regardless, your future self will thank you if you think about this early on.

Testing Methodologies (What Section)

In the popular vernacular, testing "hits different" when talking about AI. Many of you will not build ML algorithms or even fine-tune bots, but that doesn't mean we should not understand the value of testing for intention. At some point, probably in the not-so-distant future, we will all be asked to test some aspect of AI.

Because of the speed and scale and the buried layers of deep neural networks, it is irresponsible to deploy any version of an AI project without thorough testing. I've seen too many organizations that go fast and loose. I understand the pressure of being in your seat. But this is no time to make changes in production. All the bad habits you've learned along the way have to be gut-checked against what you can unleash if this gets screwed up. That is why the section on tech debt was so thorough. Testing is non-negotiable.

Formal Methods

Of course, the origin of formal verification, a subset of formal methods, comes from Alan Turing, who asked a question about our ability to check if things are right.

A Definition

"...[a] set of techniques that utilize mathematics to rigorously and efficiently analyze system behavior and prove code correctness." From the blog: Formal Methods + AI: Where does Galois fit in? April 2023

You may recall our guiding principles for using AI from a previous chapter. They include: "The ability to test concepts as well as software, algorithms or machines and reject them when they fail to meet our guiding principles." And "The ability to hold yourself and your systems accountable to real-life pressure tests to ensure performance and accuracy."

When these large systems are deployed, testing is not enough; you must verify that what you intended is what was built. Rather than fail fast, we need to validate fast.

As we have seen along the way, transparency of our systems is of the utmost importance. Not only are world governments requiring it, but organizations that are buying AI point solutions are also asking for it. If you're modifying an LLM for customization purposes, knowing exactly what is happening is difficult. As Kirsten Hoogenakker[52] told me, "It's not that easy to take feedback from the business and just go tune a hyperparameter."

But transparency is expected of us, and we should expect it of ourselves. One way to ensure that your AI solution is doing what you intend to do is through a process called "Formal Verification." Part of the long-standing practice of Formal Methods. I learned about formal verification from a TED talk.[53] Max Tegmark shared his work and answered the question we all seem to be asking, "How do we keep this thing under control?" Not only that but can we ensure that the work we're doing meets our *intentions*? I thought, "Well, that makes a lot of sense," and I was off to do research. I learned that formal verification is used a lot in semiconductors. I found little reference to its use in testing LLMs (for example).

The question about how to test and validate AI systems kept me up at night. I was deep into the writing of this book and still had no answer to this challenge. This topic requires a lot of mental capacity, and I didn't feel like I had a lot of extra capacity for reasons that have nothing to do with this book. I had stalled out and needed a reset. I had put a placeholder in this text, "Conversation with Dr. Taisa

---

[52] Kirsten Hoogenakker started off her career as a chemistry teacher who spent the majority of her time in the classroom teaching robotics and engineering. She successfully transitioned into the data and analytics space and now helps companies start AI projects. She's an advocate for thoroughness (not reactionary) in the AI space and as her LinkedIn bio says, "I provide solutions to the toughest questions."

[53] https://www.youtube.com/watch?v=xUNx_PxNHrY.

Kushner,"[54] and re-read her amazing blog post[55] in preparation.

> *"Complexity brings risk. Software and machine learning tools have never been more complex, and there has never been a greater need for the assurance and risk mitigation provided by formal methods. And yet, the vast majority of machine learning models — the very models that are revolutionizing how we interact with technology — simply do not lend themselves to formal verification. Current methods are insufficient.*
>
> *In short: cutting-edge, novel research is desperately needed to crack the code of how to apply formal methods to the machine learning puzzle."*

Then I asked Taisa, "How do you do this? What does 'novel research' mean?" Up to this point, I have had several conversations with others on this topic. There was no agreement that formal methods or formal verification would even work.

Her work at Galois (pronounced Gal-wa) is literally using formal methods to prove intent. Here's what I learned.

---

[54] Principal Researcher at Galois, an NSF Computing Innovation Fellow, and an adjunct professor at Portland State University. She also has a degree in fine arts and is the author and co-author of countless amazing blogs and scholarly papers on AI. Oh, and she's a Minnesota native too.

[55] https://galois.com/blog/2023/04/formal-methods-ai-where-does-galois-fit-in/.

These machine learning algorithms are taught on data (i.e., text, pictures, audio files, etc.). Yes, it's a lot of data, but still, it's data. And up to this point, most of the testing was to validate use cases. In other words, the model is tested with use cases that are defined by the data you used to create the model (sort of like defining a word by using the word). The only thing it does is validate the model, which has its place. But it does not address the reality of the model shifting over time (i.e., model drift[56]) and, of more concern, does not address *intent*, the hallmark of what most people worry about with AI.

Taisa and her colleagues at Galois use a novel approach by (not so simply) verifying intent using the rules or parameters of any given input. For example, let's say you create a model using data for blood pressure. Millions of rows of data go into creating the model to anticipate who will experience high blood pressure. You also use intervention data, such as when people start medication, age, weight, family history, tobacco use, all the right data points. The model is trained, and you validate it by running a couple of use cases (risk models for those more likely to need medication). All the test cases came back as expected. Are you done? Maybe not. Even if you run thousands or millions of use cases, there are potentially infinite complex real-world scenarios the model would use during deployment, and your tests might not generalize. Using formal methods, you can evaluate models on an infinite number of scenarios (including those you have not thought of), and reason about properties such as demonstrating the

---

[56] https://readwrite.com/model-drift-the-achilles-heel-of-ai-explained/.

intent of a model. You can, in fact, ensure it is doing what it was designed to do.

Think of the deep neural network as a big decision tree that branches at each yes/no answer. Rather than using a test case derived from the data used to train the model, you create a rule or parameter at each input point and branch (or node in DNN speak). This creates a graph, which is beneficial because we can understand graphs better (and often quicker) than code.[57] Rules about inputs and the values they can theoretically take on, rather than individual examples, enable you to encode an infinite number of scenarios. Follow the branches to see if it goes where you expect it to go. Once you've done this, you can probe the model and learn more about it. What interesting (graphical) patterns emerge that we didn't know about or didn't expect? You may follow one "branch" to test a specific theory, but if you were to zoom out, this branch is one small section of a much larger network of branches.

The reality is that models can also be adaptive over time. Even if you extensively test, even if you use formal methods, as you deploy the model and it uses real-world data, a model that is adaptive will shift. Anticipating that drift is important, as well as knowing what you should expect from any vendor. As we spoke about this, I asked her if she was a fan of Marvel movies. Because the obvious (to me anyway, #TeamCapForever) comparison is Vision versus Ultron. I said, "It learns *a* path not *the* path" and

---

[57] Galois actually does this for code that is not neural networks too! That is the more "classical" use of formal methods, and it is essentially creating graphs of code.

Taisa said, "Yes, exactly, and that path is very data dependent. We can verify properties, such as intent, for a model, but knowing how to define *the* path that the model *should* take is very hard." Taisa clarified, "What does it mean for an LLM to be 'correct'—very hard to define broadly though we can for specific use cases."

It was the fastest hour I've spent in a long time. It was full of information, resources, and quirky side conversations. I felt like I'd met someone important and thrilled that the universe brought us together.

Taisa, like Kirsten and Professor Mitchell before her, all said, "It (AI/ML) is meant to be a human support tool, so put a human in the center."

Eight

Governance with a Capital G

If you follow the framework and put it into practice, you will govern and manage your AI capabilities. In our data practices, we often conflate governance and management. As a matter of fact, I recently received a question from a client: "What is the difference between governance and management?" Governance is about oversight and management is about the day-to-day operations. But, when you think about data governance, for example, you do both, which is why we're often very confused about it. Words matter.

I know that the word "governance" strikes terror in the heart of a Disrupter. I get that the last thing you want to do is be slowed down while your organization figures out how to direct, control, and set accountability for AI. The good news is that you don't have to if you're a Disrupter. Let that work sit with Optimizers and Keepers while you move on to the next ideation phase (such as an innovation task force). We get into trouble when we ask Disrupters to govern, or even manage. Yet we do it all the time. A Disrupter comes up with a great idea and then you give them the responsibility to own it through delivery. Don't do that. It sets everyone up for failure. The model is sustainable because you have a mix of SDM profiles. They step in and do different things at different times, as they're best aligned to their capabilities.

Regardless of who does the work, the work has to be done. If you Google "AI Governance," you will get an amazing number of results. Go on, try it. I'll wait. Data governance has never been that popular, but you want to know a secret. They aren't that different. Yet, every vendor, government agency, quasi-government agency, consulting firm, and your grandmother's knitting club all have an AI governance framework.

I have a specific set of biases (we all do). Here's my bias about "thought leadership" and governance frameworks. If you look below the surface, many thought leaders out there have a nominal amount of applicable work experience. Before you come at me, I acknowledge that sometimes there is a ton of value in people coming from outside the field to disrupt it. It's also important to note that if you have not been living the work for the last fifteen years, you probably have a more optimistic view of the world. But I also know that social media has a way of amplifying the voices of the under-experienced. It reminds me of the Dunning-Kruger Effect,[58] stating that the less you know, the

---

[58] https://en.wikipedia.org/wiki/Dunning%E2%80%93Kruger_effect.

easier it is to talk about something. And the more you know, the less you want to talk about it. In this case, data.

As we all teeter on this AI cliff, particularly as data professionals, getting salient advice from people who have been there and done that is paramount. The trouble is very few people have "been there, done that" with AI governance. Of those out there talking about it, few have done any work in any governance. I'm not saying this to boast. I'm saying this because it's true, and we must face reality. Don't grab the first AI governance framework you see. Don't believe everything that "Thought Leader"[59] says, and please be very wary of "Influencers."[60]

The whole "Thought Leader/Influencer" thing has bugged me for a while. I do believe that, in some cases, they cause more harm than help. We don't have the luxury of spending years practicing stuff that does not work in real-world organizations. We can learn a lot from attempts at different types of governance that enterprises have tried. Every organization has several different types of governance capabilities. Let's take a look at the most frequent types of governance.

---

[59] One might refer to me as a thought leader. I've been called worse.

[60] Influencers are people that take the Dunning Kruger effect to the next level. The "I can spell AI so I'm an expert" type. Great for entertainment value, not always great for pragmatic "how-to" advice.

Governance Definitions

Access Governance[61]

Access governance (AG) is an aspect of information technology (IT) security management that seeks to reduce the risks associated with end users with unnecessary access privileges. The need for access governance has grown in significance as organizations seek to comply with regulatory compliance mandates and manage risk more strategically.

Corporate Governance[62]

Most organizations that have shareholders have a corporate governance structure. That is to say, there is a board of directors that leads the effort to manage and direct the systems, rules, practices, and processes of the enterprise. Most of us in middle management have very little exposure to this type of governance. As an aside, sitting on a board provides a great experience in learning how corporate governance works.

---

[61] https://www.techtarget.com/searchcio/definition/regulatory-compliance.

[62] https://www.investopedia.com/terms/c/corporategovernance.asp.

Data Governance[63]

Gartner's most recent definition is that "Data governance is the specification of decision rights and an accountability framework to ensure the appropriate behavior in the valuation, creation, consumption and control of data and analytics."

Another option for a definition of data governance (because I really can't say I can get behind the Gartner version). The Data Governance Institute[64] offers a few definitions as options. An old one, from the venerable "B-eye-network," is my favorite of the other options: "Data governance is the decision-making process that prioritizes investments, allocates resources, and measures results to ensure that data is managed and deployed to support business needs." It's the only one that talks about what the business needs.

Information Governance[65]

According to Wikipedia, Information Governance is defined as: "Overall strategy for information at an organization. Information governance balances the risk that information presents with the value that information provides. Information governance helps with legal

---

[63] https://www.gartner.com/en/information-technology/glossary/data-governance.

[64] https://datagovernance.com/defining-data-governance/.

[65] https://en.wikipedia.org/wiki/Information_governance.

compliance, operational transparency, and reducing expenditures associated with legal discovery. An organization can establish a consistent and logical framework for employees to handle data through their information governance policies and procedures. These policies guide proper behavior regarding how organizations and their employees handle electronically stored information (ESI).

Information governance encompasses more than traditional records management. It incorporates information security and protection, compliance, data governance, electronic discovery, risk management, privacy, data storage and archiving, knowledge management, business operations and management, audit, analytics, IT management, master data management, enterprise architecture, business intelligence, big data, data science, and finance."

Portfolio Governance[66]

"Often referred to as 'Portfolio Management,' it is the selection, prioritization, and control of an organization's programs and projects in line with its strategic objectives and capacity to deliver. The goal is to balance implementing change initiatives and maintaining business-as-usual, while optimizing return on investment." APM Body of Knowledge 7th edition as found on their website.

---

[66] https://www.apm.org.uk/resources/what-is-project-management/what-is-portfolio-management/.

Governing is a Four-Letter Word

Sometimes, I feel like governance is a four-letter word (for the record, I love four-letter words). The lack of specificity and the distraction from a myriad of sources often lead to several failed attempts. We forget that governance should equal oversight and management is the day-to-day. We forget that the touchpoint between the two must exist, yet it often doesn't. We focus on decision-rights (what) and then put them in the wrong place (who).

As I write this, my 16-year-old son is suffering from the effects of a concussion. He went snow-tubing, and, like my kid, decided to: A. not wear a helmet and B. attempt to go down the hill on his knees. After so many blissful years of parenting this magical being, countless sprains, and broken bones, I was not surprised. I will often say to him as he leaves the house, "Make good choices," knowing full well that saying that to a 16-year-old boy with a shiny new driver's license and a car is a bit like throwing an ice cube in a pot of boiling water. Pointless.

According to the government, I have two more years of full accountability for my minor child. During this time, it is my job to direct him and his behaviors, control said behaviors (often through punitive means), and hold him accountable for the behaviors. You see where I'm going with this? The reality of governing an organization full of people doing their best every day is quite similar to attempting to parent a 16-year-old boy. You need a lot of tools in your toolbox. A fair amount of diplomacy. The willingness to pivot as the need arises. Finally, some humility, as you will undoubtedly get the crap kicked out of you once in a while.[67]

Data governance has a dizzying array of definitions. The challenge is the difference between how something is defined and how something is done. When I wrote "Disrupting Data Governance," one of my primary tenets was the need to get accountability for protecting data from the day-to-day functions out of data governance. I advocated for this because most data governance professionals are recovering analysts, not regulatory or compliance professionals.

I still advise clients to have the accountability of protecting data to sit with their privacy office (or compliance, risk, etc.). There's a significant risk to your organization if you leave the protection of the data up to someone who does not have the organizational authority or the background to get the job done.

Not all governance functions are the same. What is important about any governance function is its effectiveness in real-world environments. When I work with organizations to create their data governance functions, I don't worry about defining data governance. I worry about operationalizing it. To that end, I have four pillars of data governance.

---

[67] And urban dictionary so you know what the heck he's talking about, but that probably applies more to the parenting example than the governing one. I hope.

Increasing Data Usage

I will be honest: if anything gets me worked up about data governance functions, it's when they don't focus on usage. It is the only thing that really matters when building any kind of data function. Data governance should be no different. Increasing data usage will drive support for your data governance efforts. That will bring the budget to your data governance efforts.

Improving Data Quality

There is no such thing as data governance without data quality, and there is no such thing as data quality without data governance. They are two sides of the same coin. Good data quality is the only tangible way to prove to your data consumers that data governance is working. It is difficult to know that you are doing data quality well if you don't have rules that are set with data governance. If you want to get support for data governance, focus your efforts on data quality because most organizations struggle with good or even good enough data quality.

Identifying Data Lineage

A month or so back, I presented the four pillars of data governance. Somebody in the audience asked, "Isn't data lineage another way to say metadata?" And the short answer to that is, well, sure, sort of. If I had a dime for every time an organization told me that they were collecting metadata and, therefore, they had data governance, I would be very wealthy. But metadata is not all I'm going after when I think about data lineage in the context of data governance. Data lineage encompasses metadata, but it also encompasses things like data catalogs. Data catalogs can track everything from source to target, what happens in between and how consumers see the data. How people want to use the data, such as the weights of different definitions. The ability to do a regression analysis supporting data quality remediation is important (and requires metadata).

All these things support data governance efforts. A holistic view of data as it moves along the value chain creates more value. It should not be about metadata alone.

Ensuring Data Protection

For way too long, data governance was almost solely defined by data protection or data security. Certainly, data governance has some responsibility to ensure that our assets are protected. When you perform any kind of data management function, you are responsible for protecting data. However, the reality is that the overall accountability for protecting data and the associated data assets should clearly fall under your privacy, information security, and/or compliance teams. Data governance should support this effort in two ways. First, it helps to deploy rules about the data, and second, it ensures that the actionable aspects of a policy or procedure execute within the data repository.

Data governance should not drive the creation of policies or procedures. That is the accountability of your information security, compliance, or privacy team. I encourage you to create a happy alliance with privacy, compliance, risk, and your information security team to ensure that what they do is well aligned with how you operationalize data governance in any kind of data repository.

Top Four AI Governance Considerations

Data governance evolved to be less about governance and more about management. Some of that evolution was because the protection part of data governance was pulled into an organization's legal department. That confused data governance teams with what they were supposed to "govern." With AI governance, though, there is no confusion. To govern this exciting new set of technological innovations, we must first focus on traditional governance functions of directing, controlling, and holding to account.

You get a lot of advice when you search for information on AI governance. Nothing I propose in these pages differs much from what you can find on Google, for example. It may skew towards action, though. However, we should not act without purpose or intent. But we need to catch up with what is happening in organizations worldwide.

Top-Down

AI Governance starts top-down[68] and is led by your legal department with a focus on regulatory and legislative updates. Both the AI and governance communities widely agree upon this. There is way too much happening to lead it any other way, and the risk is too great. Keepers are the answer to many of the challenges we will face in AI governance over the next three to five years.

Policies

One of the first activities of that oversight function will likely be to write policies and procedures. Lawyers are very good at documenting things. Your organization will need to comply with those policies and procedures. Some advice from someone who works a lot in organizations where governance has failed: keep the policies and procedures focused on the organization's mission. Remember, during our AI framework activities, we will dial into our own mission for the work. All those should be tied together. Remember that anything you write down and sign (ratified) becomes an official record. This means you can be audited on it, which brings me to my next consideration.

K.I.S.S. (keep it simple, silly)

Less is more. Anything you write down can become the subject of an audit. As we've explored, I don't care how you

---

[68] https://www.youtube.com/watch?v=LpNel4UL5qE.

define AI governance for your organization. What I care about is how you operationalize it. Create an oversight committee full of Keepers. Then, create an operating board full of Optimizers (with Keeper tendencies) where you keep up with documentation and specifications. But also operationalize the function with specific hand-offs.

Flexibility is Strength

It's a well-known engineering principle. In one of my conversations with Juan,[69] he ranted (his word, not mine) that we focus too much on efficiencies in most organizations. I have always preferred to talk about governance being responsive and resilient, and AI governance is no different. The only thing I can promise you over the next several years is that stuff will change. If you double down and create a very formal, too rigid governing process, you cannot keep up or innovate. That's why you must put Optimizers in the middle of this thing.

---

[69] Sure, he's the principal scientist and head of AI at data.world. Yes, the co-host of catalog and cocktails, but at his heart he's still an academic and a staunch supporter of AI in enterprises.

Time Keeps on Ticking (ticking, ticking) into the Future

We find ourselves on the cusp of such a compelling set of technology. Granted, AI has been around for decades. But it's now becoming more ubiquitous and commercialized. The governance laws that are happening today demand things like transparency, accountability, and explainability, to name a few. There's one problem with these standards. The failed logic is that most people don't understand what AI is, what machine learning is, or how to approve these technologies. All we are doing is putting layers of people "in the know" between the people creating these systems and the people most affected by them. Then, we call it governance.

In working in data governance, I have found that governance and democratization are two radically different concepts. They are the polar opposites of each other. Governance intends to stop or slow, not manage or guide. And while most of my governance friends would say that is not the spirit of the function, it is without question the result. It is also the intent of the new AI governance functions, and with good reason. Where does this leave us?

We must be clear about the function of each type of governance. That is the reason I included all the definitions. When creating our AI governance capability, we need to be clear about what we are doing and why. If we don't, we will fail at governing by conflating too many of the important, critical functions of governing AI and ignoring basic functions that support the use of data in an organization.

Governance Structure

Governance Oversight

Governance Oversight writes policies, keeps up with new legislation and regulations, functions like corporate governance structures, hand-off guidelines to Governance Operations. Primarily made up of Keepers but can have Optimizers. Should avoid Disrupters.

Governance Operations

Governance Operations focuses on ensuring there are low barriers of entry to participate with governance activities. The leaders of governance functions such as data governance come together. Primarily Optimizers and Keepers. Should avoid Disrupters.

Any project that needs governance approval to move forward. Examples may be buying an AI point solution or customizing an LLM.

Projects are brought forth through any means, from data governance or portfolio governance to individual requests. Low barrier of entry means that any person can start a conversation, send an email to request support all the way to more formal methods such as filling out forms or presenting at meetings.

Figure 8.1: Oversight, governance, directed, controlled held to account, protection full of Keepers, another box with Optimizers.

I'm a big fan of not reinventing the wheel, particularly when it comes to organization-wide changes. I spent so much time reviewing other functions of governance that are commonplace today to show that you probably have all that you need to start AI governance today. If there's anything that you do now that you can adapt, such as portfolio governance or data governance, do it.

You need to have the formality of corporate governance. The key aspects of directing, controlling, and holding to account are critical as you move toward AI. We find ourselves with shifting regulations and legislation all the time. Governance oversight that is accountable to ensure that your organization follows those laws and regulations should be the priority.

Next, you need a way to operationalize it. I've seen many failed governance functions. The one thing consistent in all those is their inability to take it from oversight (policy) to the everyday. You need people who are capable of taking those policies and operationalizing them. Think about it like governance operations.

Finally, you need a layer of AI governance that functions like day-to-day management. It's a bit like data governance and portfolio management together. Making sure that on an average Tuesday, everyone knows what to do—that the approved policies are operationalized, followed, and managed. This layer provides a lot of flexibility to your AI governance structure. It ensures that there's a formal path towards escalation if something goes haywire.

Layers are key here. In the first part of this book, we discussed the best practices in cybersecurity and their "first line of defense" standard. This governance structure allows for many lines of defense, but also attempts to remove barriers so it's easier for projects to participate in governance.

Do the Right Thing

If it were that easy to proclaim that you should do the right thing and it would be done, the world would be a very different place. In the first part of this book, I mentioned that there was a glimmer of hope not that long ago for stakeholder capitalism.[70] My generation did not put it right. We have a long way to go before telling someone to do the right thing will get the job done.

To start with, our incentives are misaligned. We can say that all stakeholders should be considered when making corporate decisions. The big decisions about what a corporation does and does not do sit with the Board of Directors. As much as we want to think stakeholders are created equal. At the end of the day, money will always win. I wish it wasn't that way, it's wrong and it should change, but that's a different book.

These misaligned incentives make it difficult to do the right thing, even if a company intends to start off right—to "not do evil things." When success comes, things get a little fuzzy. Especially when words like "accountability" fail to hold anyone accountable. I'm sure testifying in front of Congress is stressful. In the grand scheme, it's a few days, a slap on the wrist, and a few million dollars in fines for a multi-billion-dollar company. We know we have failed when failure to comply is a risk an organization is willing to take to make more money.

As we stand on this precipice of AI, our lack of ability to do the right thing is a problem. Soon, anyone can create an AI capability with the speed and scale to reach millions. Human problems cannot be solved by technology, but they sure can be propagated by it. In her book, "Data

---

[70] https://hbr.org/2023/09/what-does-stakeholder-capitalism-mean-to-you.

Conscience: Algorithmic Siege on our Humanity," Dr. Brandeis Marshall points out:

> *"People can make a choice and change their minds without notice. We can adjust on the fly given new data. Technology can't do that. It's full steam ahead for technology. The algorithms, processes, and digital systems can't reverse course. Technology, more specifically algorithms, can't determine when it may need to reconsider whether or not certain lines of code should be executed."*

There is a difference between technology companies building AI capabilities and an enterprise attempting to use AI. Proliferation is an issue. As a tech company, you intend to "go viral" to build the next big thing. That's not to say a developer in an enterprise is off the hook. Your reach may be smaller, but the intention and impact still matter. The real question is *how*? How do we hold individuals and entities responsible when "accountability" seems like a buzzword?

I came away with a core set of ideas from my readings on this topic. First, there's been a lot of attention on the ethics of AI, almost since the beginning. Yet, when taught about computer systems, computer science, or writing code, there is a shortage of curricula about the ethics of building systems.[71] Within the last five years, as AI technology has become more proliferated, governments and consulting agencies (and everyone in between) have come forth with

---

[71] Data Conscience: Algorithmic Siege on our Humanity, page 36. Brandeis Hill Marshall. Wiley 2022.

principles and guidelines. Still, we're seeing lots of questions about what's being built and concerns about its impact on humanity, and despite all the talk, there are not a lot of actionable, pragmatic tools.

A Little Less Conversation, a Little More Action, Please

Let's be clear. Conversation is important. Planning and communicating to better understand each other is a good use of time. But there comes a time when you can't talk anymore. There are no new topics. You've exhausted what you know, and it's time for action. That tipping point is so often blown right past because we're too busy talking.

I help companies build governance frameworks. I've found over the years that there are a few different kinds of enterprises and their approach to things. There are the ones that talk, and talk, and talk. They prepare PowerPoint after PowerPoint. They present at every department meeting and executive leadership session. They iterate, edit, and recast the same content in an unending array of ways. They never act. Their version of action is to find a way to talk more. Then there are the organizations that act and think later. The shoot, ready, and aim types. They seem to always be frantic about creating deliverables, anything to keep the project rolling. The focus on tactics becomes problematic when no one knows what they're doing because they're so busy doing it. It's like a canoe where everyone is rowing in the opposite direction, going around and around in circles.

It's rare for you to find an organization that balances these things well. The right amount of discussion planning against the deployment of those decisions, a few iterations with edits, and then a formal implementation. That's what we need. But most organizations can't operate that way on concrete concepts. How do we expect them to operate that way on something as abstract, layered, and challenging as AI ethics?

When I was writing my master's thesis, an advisor told me something that has stuck with me for years. You'll set out with a solid thesis and a set of assumptions and then you will discuss it, ad nauseum. You will go in several different directions, and at one point, you will be as far away from the original as possible. You know you're done (talking about it, getting advice) when you return to the original set of assumptions. Not because your original thesis was correct but because you've covered all the topics.

That's what we have to do here. We have to find that tipping point when discussing AI ethics feels like Groundhog Day—that is your sign that it's time to get to work. I've been in boardrooms and meeting rooms where this exact scenario has played out. Each time I attempt to intervene and guide. To help the company take what they've agreed on and move forward. Sometimes, I've even been successful!

I wish it were as easy as "Here's a checklist!" because who doesn't like a checklist? If it were that easy, someone would have done it by now. There is no definitive checklist, but that's what we need. As we navigate our governance layers, we must stop, or at least slow down, long enough to ask and answer some specific questions. We need to get past awareness and into tactics. Several people have come before me in this work. Of particular note for me was a paper that attempted to address the operationalization of AI Ethics.[72] In the conclusion of their paper, they stated, "...the implementation of AI ethics should be underpinned by a learning governance model where regular reflection on impact is embedded in the research and decision-making cycle and overseen by those most affected by AI..."

Think less like a hierarchal organization and more like a matrix with teams of varying SDM profiles. Our approach to governance operationalizes the "learning governance," but we still have one more thing to address. We must make certain the people in the middle of governance are the ones impacted. Putting the wrong people in the center of it may elicit the answer you want, not the one you need. You can use a product advisory group or the voice of customer groups, but the who is as important as the what.

Perhaps as you read through this, you're thinking: "This doesn't apply to me. I'm trying to bridge the gap for my data warehouse!" Doing the right thing is never easy. Asking the hard questions can bring about more work, even if you don't want to get into traditional AI projects. You can't avoid these hard questions about AI ethics. It's already happening today in every organization, and that's why this is so important. But if we all throw up our hands and say, "It's not my problem," everyone will be affected by the propagation of systematic issues inherent in our data. Because they reflect what is inherent in our world.

---

[72] https://link.springer.com/article/10.1007/s00146-021-01308-8.

It is your problem, right now.

I don't say this to scare you or prompt an angry response. When information is presented as threatening or urgent (if this, then that) it misfires in your brain. Anger isn't the response we need. Anger can light the fire, but it can't keep it going. The faster you can get through the anger, the faster you can solve the problem. Get mad. Maybe you're mad because you have to do it. Maybe you're mad because others don't or won't. Whatever the reason for your anger, get through it. We have work to do. If we all start operationalizing AI ethics, we will be in a very different place in a few years.

Know When to Hold 'em (Accountable)

Let's say that you've acquired a few point solutions, whether as part of the hodgepodge or as an attempt to use only point solutions to fill your AI strategy. How do you approach an external vendor and still hold up your set of accountabilities for doing the right thing? Whether you're building it in-house or using a vendor, some of the questions are the same:

1. Where is the data from? If they built a model, where did the data originate?

2. What guidelines did they use to acquire that data and follow regulatory best practices about privacy?

3. Did they create any data (use synthetic data)? What were the protocols?

4. What models did they use on the data? Did they start with an existing one? (LORA, GPT, etc.)

5. How do they plan to address model drift?

6. What is your ongoing plan to address model drift?

7. What governance and management structure does the vendor have to ensure they're doing the right thing?

8. What is the product roadmap? Is the company "for sale"?

9. more...

Vendor evaluation is a bit of an art form. You want to balance asking probing questions without being accusatory. Because you (probably) will have a working relationship with them at some point in the future. That said, being too "nice" means you may not ask the tough questions about what data they used, how they built the thing, and how they plan to keep your company out of the papers (and courtroom). The answer to these questions should be known long before you're close to contracting. AI vendors proliferate faster than athletes' foot in a locker room. Some of them haven't asked themselves these questions. You need to.

The Reckoning

We have established that you cannot operate out of fear—fear of being left behind or too close to the edge. Leveler heads have to prevail. The only way to bring AI thoughtfully into our organizations is through governance. I've seen up close what most organizations call governance. I've seen what they can do in the name of "governance." That's why we have to use our SDM profiles. Create a layer between traditional functions of governance and operationalization.

I have trouble with authority figures and if someone tells me what to do, I usually do the opposite to see their reaction. That's my core operating procedure. But I've lived long enough in corporate America to know that sometimes, we must create methods, rules, and structures that keep us on the right path.

One of AI's biggest promises and its biggest peril is the speed of scale. We must find a way to govern aspects of this, not to stifle it, but to ensure a straight path full of equal promise (and no harm).

Nine

Welcome to the Real World

What does happen when people stop being polite and start getting real?

Theory is great. To be honest, some of this is theoretical, but I've seen a lot of it play out in the real world through my work. Using a real-life framework is different from writing one for a book. My favorite books are the ones that get right to the point, the ones that I read and walk away thinking, "I can do that!"

A lot is holding us back from jumping into AI projects, from organizational structures and tech debt to a lack of documentation and skills. There's probably some pent-up organizational demand. Sure, we have data and smart people. Most of your data is probably in the cloud. But just because you have many of the things it takes to "do AI" doesn't mean you can. It's a little like buying a Cessna 152 (that's a small two-person airplane) and turning it into a rocket ship. Yes, they both fly. They have engines and are aerodynamic, but that might be where the similarities end.

Let's look at the issues that will hold you back and what to do about them. This is a little like me airing my grievances about the data industry. It's been very cathartic.

I Wanna Push You Around

Sometimes, when you're leading a team, taking action is impossible. Sometimes, you're weighed down by your previous decisions or the decisions of a previous leader. Another way to think about that is tech debt. Tech debt can be like Marley's chains.

Past you has created a problem for future you.

Maybe you're getting a ton of pressure to develop an AI strategy. Maybe you know it's time to start thinking about team structure and skills gaps. Then you see the tech debt, how much your organization has created, and the maintenance nightmare you live in, which gives you pause. Give in to that feeling, take a hot minute, and assess your tech debt before you add a speed and scale function like AI to your repertoire. Part of being future-ready means you cannot propagate tech debt like it's your job. Your mantra should be, "There's nothing more permanent than a temporary solution." I have seen this play out more times than I can count, and the tech debt spiral happens for many reasons.

It's Not Me It's You

A few years ago (time is relative, you know?), I was working with a start-up that had a ton of buzz. It was exciting to play a small part in it. They had passed several series funding levels with flying colors. As I was sitting in a non-descript conference room with two of the executives, I felt a tinge of "Uh oh." I don't know how to explain this other than to say that after working in data for over twenty years, I can tell you in the span of a few hours what is wrong. Some of it is being an objective third party and some of it is experience. I've had the innate gift for a while now. I try not to terrify people when I first meet them, though. I've found that I don't get far if I blurt out, "You're the problem!" Despite my reputation, I often work hard to soft-pedal that news. Sure, sometimes that doesn't work, and I have to say in no uncertain terms what is wrong, plain language, bordering on lacking tact (gasp). But as I was sitting in that conference room at that moment, I thought I could help them.

Fast forward six months. I had been toiling away in the trenches with front-line leaders (I love it there), but it did feel like we got shot at every time we stuck our heads out. We tried to build repeatable frameworks and create boundaries with hand-offs, but all we got was, "Yeah, that's great. Is it done yet?" Their version of propagating tech debt was the pressure they were under to build. This meant that they often decided to create something with duct tape and chicken wire without consideration for long-term use. The company, which was a few years old and had such buzz, was built on nothing solid. I did have a tough conversation with the executive. But reality being what it is, even those conversations didn't go far. He knew the problem, but because of the organizational demands, he was thwarted from fixing them. One of the hardest things to do as a company advisor is knowing that you can help but walk away anyway because they aren't ready or capable.

Tech debt happens for many reasons, but I've seen my fair share of poor Agile deployment topping that list. Don't get me wrong, I'm a huge fan of Agile. When done right, the way you get stuff done can change. But this is the real world, after all. In this case, a few executives read an article about Agile. They read about the "small Agile teams" and thought "more with less" and ran with it. True Agile methods, regardless of your particular flavor, are not about haphazardly throwing crap out the door. When done well, they are actually more thought through and documented than most projects using other methods. Yet, often, organizations end up with Agile deployments that spool tech debt.

Another tech debt creator that's high on my list is lack of leadership. I know some of you reading this are going to take offense. I have worked for a charismatic leader more than once in my career. Someone who is inherently likable. When you combine that with an amiable personality, not much good comes from that, at least not as a technology or data leader. I don't mean to imply that you have to be a jerk. You can be likable, even amiable, but you must stand up for your team and prevent stuff from rolling downhill. Being a data leader in a modern organization is a tough job. The pressure comes from all sides; no matter what you do, it's never enough. I understand the inclination to over-promise, soothe the raging stakeholder, and grease that squeaky wheel. Sometimes, that's all you can do, but when that's all you do, you have a problem.

I remember working once with a tech leader who was great in the boardroom. He was clear and concise and never talked down to people about the complexities of the technology. He always had an answer. His peers loved him, but the people that worked under him did not feel the same way. It was day after day of shifting priorities, urgent requests, and lack of direction. His ability to manage the boardroom meant he capitulated to almost every request. Even the ones that were in no way possible. Front-line leaders would get an angry email from someone who expected a deliverable they didn't even know about and were forced to build something quickly. Tech debt proliferated, and the more we created, the more we had to maintain. Maintaining poorly created technology is much more work than when you have the time to build it right the first time. Pretty soon, the whole IT department was buried under buckets of maintenance, with no time to build new equipment or do it right. It took years, but eventually, it caught up to that executive, and the boardroom started asking some serious questions.

Whether it is an amiable personality or the inability to stand up to the deluge of demands, a lack of leadership is a fast track to tech debt. No organization in the world is large enough, with the right people and all the financial resources to build everything they want. The word "No" is a full sentence and saying it is part of the job. Use it judiciously, of course. You can't say no to everything but must say no sometimes.

You hear a lot about "data literacy" in the data industry. I don't know when it popped up. I do recall writing about it for the first time in my second book, "Data Driven Healthcare," and at the time, I felt like it was the answer to many questions. As people do, however, the hype around data literacy has become a mantra. "I could do it all if I had only had high data literacy in my organization." Friends, that's a load of crap.

We have used data literacy as a crutch and an excuse for too long. Having a completely naïve, incompetent team would indeed make it difficult to deploy data insights. Spoiler, no one has that. You have a team full of competent professionals *with different skill sets*. It's not everyone's job to "get data," and your stakeholders are not dumb. The lack of understanding in your organization sits on your shoulders (as the data leader), not anyone else's. At the core, that is what "data literacy" should be about. Instead, it has turned into a reason not to deliver.

Maybe it's because we call it data literacy, implying that these competent professionals are illiterate. Even if it were true, who would want to be called illiterate? When you have failed to fill in the gaps for your organization, it is possible that their lack of understanding makes your job harder. It's also feasible that it increases tech debt because they lack the understanding to support the work, to understand that it takes the time it takes. Build a team of champions that can help you spread the word. Everyone wants to be a champion ("We are the champions, my friends").

One final note on data literacy. As the LLMs become more commercialized, the ability to prompt and get answers on even structured data will become commonplace. The need for data literacy programs geared towards business stakeholders to create knowledge to interact with complex or convoluted data completely disappears. In its place, a prompt box that can answer multi-layered questions like, "What was the impact of the product rollout in quarter two?" or "Did the west region do better than the east region in sales?" These next-generation AI systems can answer questions in normal, natural language with data tables and visualizations.

Figure out what your organizational dynamic is that has created a high amount of tech debt. Once you have identified it, the second step is to figure out how to fix it. Muscle memory is a tough thing. If your organization has been operating this way for a long time, it will take effort to undo it. Start a campaign that allows you to surface why tech debt occurs. Isolate the behaviors that continue to propagate it. Create a plan to start deprecating the tech debt. You don't have to be done with it to start your AI journey, but you better have a plan not to make it worse.

Mad Skills

We talked about the organizational structure in Chapter Six. Now, we're going to address upskilling. Your average data team member probably doesn't have many baseline "AI" skills. That's also true in reverse, that most AI developers started that way. If you're looking to become future ready, you have to be willing to invest in your people and their skills.

It's not only about technical skills, either. Right now, I can go out to ChatGPT and have it write me a query in Python code. It is worth the effort to ensure your data team has a basic understanding of AI and all that comes with it. Several courses, varying from free to very expensive, can address that need. You also have some specific skill sets that will need to change. Each person will approach this in a different way, and you have to meet them where they are at, to some degree. I'd recommend creating individual training plans. Each person should create their own based on some set ground rules that you have set for the team. Knowing their SDM profile will help inform their natural inclination toward new things. Part of that training plan should be some upskilling in change management. You're introducing an enormous amount of change in your organization, even if you don't reorganize your team or take any of the other pieces of advice. You're still introducing a new technology that will disrupt everyone's life. Change management should be part of the upskill plan to ensure everyone has the tools to navigate the shifts.

Start with your AI roadmap. Identify a timeline when most need to complete their upskill plan. Then, ask each person to complete their own upskill plan. This is valuable because you likely have more Keepers and Optimizers on your team. Those Keepers will have a harder time with the changes, so you must give them more time. If you know that in 18 months, you will be deprecating something a Keeper built, it's safe to say they will take 24 months to come along. When you know that ahead of time, it won't feel so frustrating in the moment. When you plan for it, creating expectations across the organization is more feasible.

I Do Not Think it Means What You Think it Means

Yes, you need good data for AI. But let's break that down a bit, shall we? First, "AI" is a tiny acronym filled with all kinds of misnomers and misunderstandings. You can't just "Do AI," it's not like strapping on some running shoes.

I've seen lots of posts about how AI requires good data. And it does. That is indisputable. Then I started to wonder how in the world we were going to figure this out. Because the fact is most organizations don't have "good" data. Lamenting it does not change the fact that after decades of advice, guidance, and outright begging, we are nowhere near where we need to be.

Obviously, someone at some point had good enough data to create LLMs. Then, I realized we have a bit of a chasm in the data industry. During the research for this book, I realized that the AI/ML researchers of the world used language that almost every data team in organizations use. Yet, the definition of them is vastly different. We all use terms like "big data," "data science," and "data lake." There are two branches of the data industry, and we're confused about terms and roles.

The primary difference between the two, data for industry and AI/ML research data, is intention and incentives. When you work in a data team for an enterprise, any enterprise from a large retail store like Target to Jim's Body Shop, your primary directive is to move at the speed of business. When working in a data team for AI/ML in your Big Tech companies, your primary directive is to get the model right. Getting those models (for example, GPT 3.5) took decades. It took trillions of rows of text from all kinds of places. No enterprise has that, or even if they did, they would not have had the patience to allow it to take decades to see value.

Data for Industry		Data for AI/ML Research
The five "Vs"	Big Data	Trillions of rows of data
Someone who can take the data wherever it is and answer questions	Data Science	Someone who can take the data and create a model
An architectural principle in which you take similar types of (usually structured) data and drop it into "tables," then you apply transformations to clean it so it can be used for reports.	Data Lake	Take any data from any source. Create concepts or domain types. Drop the data (any data type, structured, unstructured, or semi-structured) in the closest concept table. Then use that data to feed the model.
We have no choice but to go fast, and it shows.	Reality	They had no choice but to get it right and it took decades.
Totally different intentions and incentives.		

Figure 9.1: Data for Industry Type.

Psychic Friends Network

In 1993, I was on a break from college. I had enrolled at a community college to get my first two years cheaper since I had to pay for it on my own. I was still working full-time and had burned myself out. I was having some health issues and needed surgery, so late-night TV was sort of my thing. Between 1993 and 1994, the Psychic Friends Network[73] commercial with the now-infamous Miss Cleo[74] aired 12,000 times. I'm pretty sure I saw 11,999 of those. Miss Cleo and the other psychics knew all. They could tell you your past, future, and that secret you had been keeping for a small fee per minute. I would imagine that if you have a team of psychics and mind readers, then documenting your work wouldn't be necessary. For the rest of us, I'm sorry to say, you have to write stuff down. I get that documentation is not your favorite part of the job. The reality is that without documentation of what you did (and sometimes why you did it), you're only doing half the job. Documentation helps you create repeatability for your function. It means you can take a vacation or a promotion because someone else can step in and do what you do.

The good news? Now, there's software that can support you in your efforts. I'm not an advocate for documentation for documentation's sake. There's a minimum threshold you should meet, but after that, it's up to you. If you want to scale and be future-ready, part of that has to be

---

[73] https://en.wikipedia.org/wiki/Psychic_Friends_Network.

[74] https://www.rottentomatoes.com/m/call_me_miss_cleo.

memorializing the work. It allows others to step in when you're on vacation, too busy, or leave the company.

When you're a Hammer

The default for most organizations is to build a data repository because that's what we do. I'm not saying you don't need to do that. I am saying, don't assume you do. Something is to be said for the tried and true, but value should be at the top of your mind. I've seen a lot of data repositories over the years. Not all of them were valuable, and many became expensive distractions. If you're at a place where you haven't built anything yet, I recommend you start challenging some conventions. No question should be off-limits when you're building towards a future-ready platform. Find a Disrupter in your organization and let them loose on the plan. See what options they come up with. The rule of the day is what value it provides and how long that will take. If you're looking at two years before you see value in the repository, and you're proposing you do that before you start your AI journey, I'm going to venture to guess that's too long.

Winter is Coming

It is January in Minnesota. Although I've traveled all over, I've lived my entire life in the great North, from Wisconsin to North Dakota to Minnesota. I love the winter. I love the cold. Most people who aren't from here don't understand that winter is a crucial part of our lifecycle. We spend a lot of the year planning for it. Yes, you can look out onto the desolate landscape and wonder how anything could survive. Then spring happens, and you see the plants and animals pop up, stronger than ever. Winter is an important part of rest. That rest gives us time to think about where we want to spend the spring. Plan for how we will survive summer.

I recently read a LinkedIn post by my friend Juan Sequeda about an impending AI winter. AI enthusiasts and experts alike are terrified of this. There have been two significant AI winters in the past. Each follows a cycle of hype around what AI could do, then some big rounds of investments to prove it. Promptly followed by a fall from grace when they failed to deliver the goods. AI winters vary in severity and length, like the ones in Minnesota, and are inevitable.

Are we on the precipice of an AI winter? I don't like trying to predict things. It seems like a fool's errand. But the ingredients are there. The hype for AI right now is off the charts. It is in your face everywhere you go. Everyone, from my elderly father to the ladies behind me in the coffee shop to my 12-year-old niece, talk about it like they're experts. So, hype—check. Next is investment. Companies and investment strategists alike are investing billions in the gold rush. Every organization that does *anything* with data is "investing" in AI. To avoid an AI winter, the Value > Hype + Investment. Unfortunately, I don't know how this is possible because the hype is too high. AI enthusiasts are worried, but I see an AI winter as a good thing.

We need a minute. It's time to take a beat. We have to slow down long enough to understand where the value is (spoiler: not in a chatbot). We have to assess what the appropriate investment is. We need to show value that's beyond the productivity gains of chatbots. Don't get me wrong, I like chatbots. Moxy built one for our website to let people interact and ask questions about data governance. We also use ChatGPT to help with our marketing. They both created a productivity boost, to be sure. Our investment (therefore, risk) was very small. But, as we have seen, the equation has to balance. I should not invest a ton of money without value, and I shouldn't invest a small amount of money and expect huge gains.

Commercializing AI, which is what we're trying to do now, will take time to do right. We don't yet understand what AI is, what it can do for us, or what amount of investment is right. We have a lot of foundational ground to cover. I think an AI winter gives us the time to do that. To rest a minute and decide how we want to spend our spring.

Bitter with the Sweet

We all live in the real world. Data teams and functions are not always a solid foundation for AI deployment in the real world. If your tech debt is already holding you back, it will no doubt be a problem when AI comes into town. If you lack skills on your team or have no documentation, these things will also present problems. As exciting as the new stuff is, you must fix some old problems.

Ten

Step by Step

If you've made it this far, congratulations. Up to this point, I've given you a lot to think about and some amorphous ideas on how to get started. In this last section of the book, I will try to get prescriptive about how to start and be as precise as possible. The focus is on reusable methods and plans that many types of organizations can use. Of course, there are always nuances, so I share a few case studies at the end of this section.

We need a couple of definitions before we get started. Throughout these pages, we've referred to "AI" in a very general sense. However, as we learned in the first part of this book, there are different types of AI. Before we can talk about what it means to incorporate AI into your data journey, we need to know what "AI" we're talking about. A quick Google search revealed anywhere from four[75] [76] to seven accepted types of AI. Our ChatGPT answer had two broad categories of AI. Part of the challenge with AI is the lack of consistency in what we are referring to.

Reactive AI
Task Specific, such as pattern recognition. Faster than any human because it's a machine. But not great at anything that falls outside of its narrowly defined scope.

Limited Memory Machines
Good at complex tasks and classifications. It can take on data and "get smarter" (the algorithm adjusts as data changes). This is the current state of AI.

Theory of Mind
Machines understand motives and reasoning. A high degree of personalization. Uses less data because it understands intent. It is theoretical, nothing has been built yet.

Self-Awareness
This doesn't exist, but it seems to be what the goal is and where we are heading (insert incredulous shrug here). It is the sci-fi version of AI. It will sense and predict, think Vision (before the body) in Marvel. Or Ultron, which seems to be an equally possible result.

---

[75] https://www.techtarget.com/searchenterpriseai/tip/4-main-types-of-AI-explained.

[76] https://www.coursera.org/articles/types-of-ai.

What's your Type?

Because we're focusing on organizations already on their data journey, we need to identify the boundaries of what an AI project could mean. We know we live in the "Limited Memory Machines" part of AI. Beyond that, though, it is ill-defined. Much of AI has been focused on language because so much is communicated via words.[77] The paltry amount of structured data doesn't interest the researchers as much. Based on my research, most "AI for structured data" isn't AI. We've also seen a lot of AI-washing[78] because of the hype.

What constitutes AI is a little fuzzy. I'm going to propose some basics that are required for creating "AI" from scratch. So, when your executive comes up to you and says, "Let's do AI!" rather than thinking of how quickly you can update your resume, you can feel better prepared. To begin, we need lots of data (big data, as it were). Then, because you have big data, we will need computing power. Usually, it is in the cloud because you need a lot and the ability to scale with ease. And last but not least, powerful statistical methods. If you use this as a litmus test, in most cases, enterprises will not rise up to the definition of AI. This is an important distinction. Even if you can build an AI strategy, you may not be able to build AI.

---

[77] https://bigcloud.global/what-is-unstructured-and-structured-data/#:~:text=Estimates%20suggest%20that%20around%2080, world's%20data%20is%20currently%20unstructured.

[78] https://www.wsj.com/articles/sec-head-warns-against-ai-washing-the-high-tech-version-of-greenwashing-6ff60da9.

Your AI strategy should include utilizing all the data in your enterprise. Much of what exists in your average operational system, such as a CRM, is semi or unstructured data. The work of the algorithms common today in AI (LLMs) is about making words into code so the machine can read them. Helping us navigate lots of unstructured and semi-structured data with ease. This is why semantic models have a leg up. Most organizations have spent their time dealing with structured data. Assuming that you have that down, we must focus on bringing all data types together.

Most of the world's data (approximately 80%), falls into these two categories, unstructured or semi-structured, such as text, visuals, or audio files.	The remainder of the data (approximately 20%), is what most data repositories were built on, structured data (i.e., numerical data)

Figure 10.1: Data Types.

From the Top

I propose you start with the SDM profiles. In Chapter 7, three sets of questions relate to the sustainable disruption model: Disrupter, Optimizer, or Keeper. Have everyone in your data team self-evaluate. Some organizations have found completing the questions and discussing their "fit" for each person valuable. Once you know the overall profile of your team, you know what might be missing or skewed. Also, consider the SDM profile for anyone participating in these AI projects. That could include parts of IT, business departments, and governance.

Missing You

Let's say you complete the profiles and see you have a big gap, one you know will become a problem. There are a few tricks I've learned that I'll share with you. First, everyone will likely have a primary and a secondary part of their SDM profile. In a pinch, you can use the secondary profile to fill the gap. For instance, say you're missing a bunch of Optimizers. But you have several people that have that as their secondary profile. You can use them as if they were Optimizers. It's not a long-term solution. Keep in mind that not all secondary profiles are created equal. If you have someone who is a strong Disrupter with a bit of Optimizer mixed in, don't expect them to focus on "optimizing." The same goes for someone who heavily associates themselves as a Keeper. To be helpful, that secondary profile should be strong as well.

You might find some skews in your team even when utilizing secondary profiles. That's pretty common because people like to hire people like themselves. Data tends to attract Keepers, so if you're missing Keepers, you can borrow Keepers from other teams for certain functions. Typically, you can borrow them long enough to help you understand what they would do if they were on the team. In other words, that borrowed Keeper will help you see the things you're missing. As I've said before, Keepers are the bedrock of sustainable disruption. Don't ignore missing Keepers.

Missing Optimizers can also present some big problems, especially if your team profile is bimodal with lots of

Disrupters and Keepers. I'm going to bet that you are experiencing some chaos. The Optimizers bridge that gap so seamlessly that most of us don't even realize what they are doing until they're gone. Up to this point, I'm assuming you can't hire people. Now is a great time to look for an Optimizer if you can. You could also look to a consultant or contractor to fill that void. I haven't seen a lot of scenarios where you can borrow Optimizers. They tend to be very embedded in their work because of the bridge-building. Most team leaders don't want to risk losing them. If you can borrow one to help you in the short term, great.

Finally, there's the scenario where you're missing Disrupters. In truth, that's the easiest one to tackle. If you're in a place where you're not creating new stuff, then you don't need a Disrupter. Missing one isn't a big deal. Since you're reading a book about bringing AI into your organization, it's safe to assume that there's a need for Disrupters on your team. Of the three profiles, Disrupters are the easiest ones to hire as a short-term consultant or contractor.

As we learned earlier, Disrupters can be tough to work with because they're always disrupting. Creating a situation where you contract someone for a short period to fill that void makes a lot of sense. One word of caution. Let them do their job. Don't spend a lot of money having a consultant fill the Disrupter gap only to ignore them. We all need a balance, and Disrupters must be part of it.

Tech Debt Deprecation Plan

High degrees of tech debt will stand in your way. You need to reduce it as much as you can. I'd love to say get rid of it, but that's not always feasible. Keepers and Optimizers will be a good fit for this work. You have to identify the type of tech debt you have. Create an inventory of all things that you would consider to be tech debt. Then figure out how they happened. We first need to identify the pattern (or patterns) outlined in Chapter 9. Create a plan to not only fix the problematic tech but also to stop its proliferation.

In many cases, it might be easier to fix the tech than fix the reason you got into debt. Isn't that just the way? No one likes to air their dirty laundry. You can ask a friend for help if you're struggling with this. Sometimes, someone outside the team can identify the dynamic faster than one inside.

If your tech debt is due to the enormous pressure to get stuff done, that's a leadership problem. Ask your executive leader. If you don't have a CDO, then it's the first-line executive to whom your team reports. When I say executive here, I mean someone with a seat at the table, not someone with a title. So, unfortunately, if your CDO is only in title, you still have to seek out that executive with influence. Explain the impact of all the tech debt. You should have numbers in either hours or dollars to back that up. Then, have a very specific ask. Not "I need your help to stop it." Rather, "The pressure that is coming in from the executive layer to do more with less is unsustainable. We cannot be successful if we continue this way. We need (pick one) "clear, laser-like focus on a direction." Or "we need more resources (be specific about type and cost)." Or "we need more time (again be specific)." Others are missing here, but you get the general point.

The hardest tech debt creator? Poor leadership. I don't have a quick tip for that. Especially if the "poor" part of that leadership is your executive. That's a tough conversation—it's not impossible, but tough. It may be worth trying to have a conversation that shares your concerns in a clear and concise but kind way. Try to avoid getting so frustrated you blurt it out. Plan the discussion points and practice with someone you trust. The leader may not even know they are the problem. Remember to be specific. Don't use generic references like, "Your amiable personality creates tech debt!" Rather, "Last week, you told Raj we could complete his request in three days. Two weeks ago, you told Ashley that her request could be completed in 10 days. In neither of those instances did you check with the teams. In both cases, the teams have had to scramble, drop other stuff, and not build it in a way that can avoid tech debt. How can we avoid this in the future?"

If your tech debt results from a bad Agile deployment, fix your Agile methods. There is an unending array of resources on this topic. My friends at DataKitchen have great stuff on all things "Ops" if you need help there. If you need help with Scrum, check out Scrum Inc. The key with Agile is not less with more. It is stripping away the extraneous and focusing on delivering value-added work. If you're not doing that, then ask yourself why.

Please don't ignore your tech debt. It will haunt you forever. The Appendix contains a version of a tech debt deprecation plan (TDDP).

Tech Debt Depreciation Plan				
ID	Title	Description	Category	Priority
101	Hardcoded Nightmare	An urgent request came in (had less than 24 hours) to set up the password expiration. The developer felt they had to hardcode the expiration time which means that if the business requirements change in the future (e.g., if the company decides that password reset links should expire after 48 hours instead of 24), developers will need to revisit and modify the code again.	Lack of configurability	2
102	Poor Code Quality	A quick implementation of the software involved shortcuts or hacks that sacrifice code readability, maintainability, or extensibility. This can lead to increased bugs, difficulties in debugging, and slower development in the future.	Quick and Dirty	1

Figure 10.2: Tech Debt Deprecation Plan.

Moving On, Letting Go

It's time to move your data team into a business department. As we've already explored, leaving the data team in IT misaligns the function with its intent. So much of what we need to know to deliver great work is within the business departments. That's not to say the move won't be hard. It's the right thing to do, but it's still a challenge.

This realignment will best position the data team to provide value-added deliverables that will sync with the business as your enterprise builds your AI strategy. The churn you could create here could be significant. I recommend pulling people out of other teams if they do a lot of data work. Sometimes, that can feel like a "land grab." I do not advocate for large data teams, particularly if they're dysfunctional. You need to pull together all the people who work with data if your organization is going to start an AI journey.

The arguments about centralizing and decentralizing data teams have been going on forever. I believe many conversations about centralizing and decentralizing are false choices. They are just two different options that service distinct functions. We have to keep in mind that good is what works and bad is what doesn't work. So, whether or not you're centralized or decentralized matters only if it works. Centralize when you need to coordinate functions to create a repeatable method of working. When it's decentralized, the work brings people along with you. That's fine if you're not in a build phase. When you need to move fast, taking the time to bring people together can feel too time-consuming. Too often, it gets skipped. When you skip it, you violate one of the core tenets of change management: awareness. The straight answer is that if you're trying to build fast, it is easier to centralize those people together. Once you're out of that build phase, decentralize everything you want. One important note on the whole centralized/decentralized thing is that the argument often existed because the decentralized model meant that some data and analytic resources went to the business lines. They will all be in our re-org.

Oversight and Operations

Next up, you will need to get an AI governance board going. Pick the people from compliance, risk, privacy, and information security with a heavy focus on Keepers. Setting the tone for a top-down, "We are serious about doing AI right," communication. Many of these things will run in parallel to take the best advantage of time. How long this will actually take is completely up to your organization. If your culture is one of dragging its feet and not adopting new things, then it could take ages.

> History will be kind to those who thoughtfully
> prepared and executed expeditiously.

Governance should start with a charter. Define scope, create policies, and identify the boundaries and hand-offs to governance operations. The oversight board will also issue guidelines for what constitutes an AI project. Identify what boundaries exist between governance, oversight, and projects. Knowing that hand offs helps you move faster.

Hand offs to governance operations are the differentiator to this approach. Too often, it gets lost somewhere in the governance function. Here we are calling it out. Adapt methods from portfolio governance to keep value at the heart of everything we do. The operational aspect of AI governance will create procedures (based on policies) and standardize tools, methods, and workflows. If governance and management are two gears, the operations are like silicone lubricant. One key element of the operations function is reducing the barrier to participating in governance. In most organizations, projects will avoid governance because they don't want to be slowed down. When a project gets the go-ahead, there's usually a timeline associated with it. Agile coaches and project managers consider their success rate defined by their ability to deliver on time. The governance operations group makes participating in AI compliant and safe, with low barriers for projects to keep their timelines.

A Better Future

At the center of this, the reason why we're spending all this time and resources is to prepare for AI projects. After re-aligning your data team and creating your governance structure, it's time to decide how to approach your future. The exciting thing about being "future-ready" is that it is more of a mindset than dogma or technology. You may know exactly how you want to do this or which option makes the most sense. But if not, create a pros/cons list. It can help you decide. We're creating a set of principles by which your organization lives. That helps to ensure that no matter what the future brings, you can pivot.

We will follow the framework as we start to kick off based on your future-ready plan. Each project will have its own set of criteria and steps. Following the framework means you have easier hand-offs to governance operations, making it quicker and easier to get the all-clear to move ahead with the project. As you build the layers of oversight and operations, there should be no confusion about who does what when. Create repeatable, consistent methods of onboarding projects, with stated intent, business values or goals, data sources, and transparency of models. Onboard people with pre-defined training and provide standards of participation.

Your organization should make change management a cornerstone of your AI journey. Thanks to the hype, media, fake news, deep fakes, and all the rest, people are terrified of AI. This will touch every job. Our only parallel in recent history is the personal computer, which took decades to roll out and become ubiquitous. We're on the fast track. Helping your people understand and come to terms with AI is paramount. The entire organization must know that you are doing this correctly. You're not throwing something on the wall to see if it will stick. You're starting with governance, with a mission and vision. You've asked yourself, your peers, and each project: "What happens if we're successful?" Share these messages with everyone in your enterprise as you start this exciting new journey.

How to Deploy the Framework

In Chapter 7, we reviewed a framework and how to complete the document. Now, we will go over how to deploy it. Think of frameworks like plans—they only work if you work them, and that's what we're going to do now.

As a reminder, the framework covers who, what, when, how, and how much. You know your "who" because you (should have) spent time completing SDM profiles. The "what" section represents the future-ready data type you've decided on. Writing that into your framework document is the easy part. Now we have to figure out "how" to deploy.

Create, Cultivate, Collaborate, Communicate[79]

How we work will vary from organization to organization. However, each enterprise needs to address the following functions: Create, Cultivate, Collaborate, and Communicate. Regardless of how you plan on approaching your future-ready, you need each.

Getting started means you have to create some documentation. Governance has already created its charter

---

[79] Feel free to hum the Inxs Mediate tune, I tried to include it in here, but it just didn't fit.

and policies. As the project team, you will need to create documented use cases. Be able to address questions about data and where it comes from. You will also need to identify what technology you intend to use (if a point solution is part of the plan). Working with governance operations, these documents help you move through the governance layers quickly.

As you move past the initial phase of use cases, you must start cultivating your backlog. Whether it's a POC or a pilot, there are steps to iterate. Treat this phase as you would any other project. A network of supporters or champions attached to the use cases will be valuable. You don't want to do this in a vacuum, and data teams have historically had a bad reputation for doing this. The only way to successfully navigate bringing AI into your organization is if you bring people with you. Speaking of bringing people with you, collaborating is a big part of executing. Collaborations will be made with your governance teams, information security, and key stakeholders.

I hope I have reiterated this enough, but in case I haven't, communication is a hallmark of change management. Hiring or dedicating a resource to it would be valuable if you can. From the beginning, you need to communicate your vision. Don't shy away from sharing the appropriate information. If people hear about it as part of the organization's grapevine, they will assume you're hiding something for a reason. The amazing thing about communication is someone will fill in the holes if you don't do enough of it. What they share may not be accurate, but they will be first. That first piece of information is one people tend to believe. Your ability to move through these phases at a quick pace is dependent on your ability to communicate. I've seen so many programs fail because they didn't communicate enough or at all.

As you operationalize your framework, you will see that I missed stuff. That is bound to happen. The analogy I use a lot is board games. I am not a fan of board games—I find them boring. We have an international exchange student. He loves board games. I've found myself playing more of them since his arrival. All the games were new to me, which meant that I had to read the instructions or have someone explain the game to me. I've tried both. Nothing worked as well as reading the instructions and playing the game. The same is true for a lot of projects. Be thoughtful and prepare well. Then, play the game. Be ready to pivot and adjust. Add helpful documents. Skip stuff that doesn't make sense for your organization. I'm not advocating a "fast and loose" approach, at least not across the board. But there is no better teacher than experience.

Examples

In this section, we will apply all we have learned to three different use cases. Each of these are real-world people and organizations taking on disruptive change. Not all these changes were AI, but they were informative enough to use them in this capacity.

Starting from Zero Got Nothing to Lose

This is a story of how not to do things. We often learn the most from these types of situations. We will learn what happened and then apply some of our recommendations to recast the past.

The startup life. There's nothing like it. The mission, the excitement, the money (lack of or rolling in it depending). Our case study is a startup in the mental health field. They plan to use data from call centers, sleep data, and self-reported data from apps to predict and then intervene with appropriate care recommendations. A lot of excitement has built up around this company. Several series of funding attempts later, they had broken through. Now they have funding and a lot of pressure.

They were the belle of the ball as soon as the series funding happened. The CEO was being interviewed and presented as the next Disrupter in mental health. The app, with its AI capabilities, was called a game-changer. A lot of what was in the press got them more interest from investors, but a lot of it wasn't true. That's when the pressure hit. People started to expect them to have a finished product. But the funding was to *create* the product. They had tested several applications and knew where to start, but that was it.

Because she hadn't delivered, the board replaced the CEO. And is often the case, the new CEO hired a new team. The pressure to create something presented them with two options. Build it or buy it. They chose to buy it. They thought they could onboard consultants much easier than they could hire. They found a consulting company that could build the architecture. They found another one to serve as data scientists and still another to be the product managers. In the beginning, it seemed to be working. Progress was quick, and each group worked to create their deliverables. When it came time to present to the board, it was obvious that there was no cohesion between the three functions.

The product team had great ideas but no data to back it up. The architecture team created something that wouldn't support the product ideas. It also didn't support what the data scientists wanted. Nobody thought to start with what data we could actually get, either through buying or partnering with other companies. The three consulting companies that had these three distinct jobs rarely talked with each other. There was no plan or cohesion, and at this point, the startup had spent a lot of money and had almost nothing to show for it. You would think this is where they would stop and assess and not repeat past mistakes. You would be wrong. They hired another consultant to be the bridge-builder (yours truly).

I was excited by the idea. I started off my career in the mental health field, and as I toured their facilities, it brought it all back. The architect drew what he was building on the whiteboard. Nothing existed yet because he didn't have data. It was theories about tables that might work if they had the data they needed. The product manager shared what she was creating. PowerPoints, which had compelling stories and mocked up apps on phones. None of it real, none of it feasible. The data scientist phoned in to share his insights. He had good research and applicable stuff, if they had the data and the tech to commercialize it, which they didn't. It was pretty obvious to me what was needed, and frankly, it wasn't me.

We were brought in to help ease the communication between product and architecture. Build some dashboards to show that they had *something* they could use to prove they had done work. I'd like to tell you that I fixed everything. I didn't. Sometimes, dynamics are too deeply embedded. Hindsight is so much clearer than when you're living in it. I told them they needed an employee with different, more aligned goals to lead the charge. I also told them that fewer consulting companies would make staying on top of the work easier. Then the hard part, I had to tell them that what they wanted and what was feasible were two different things. The data didn't exist, and even if it did, there wasn't enough data to predict behaviors. The relationships between the variables were tenuous. They would need a lot more money (and computing power) before they could prove it.

The disappointment was palpable. They tried for several more months to push that rock up the hill. Eventually, the board stepped in. Replaced the leadership (again) and tried to get more funding. Their doors shuttered a few months later.

A Different Outcome

What would happen if we were to recast that story with the things we've learned so far? First, we would look at the SDM profile of the people involved. Disrupters seemed to be leading the charge, bulldozing through pesky details like feasibility and operational effectiveness. Suppose we start at the beginning with the Disrupter who had a great idea. In our fictitious scenario, she was smart enough to see her limitations. Rather than instilling herself as CEO, she hired an Optimizer and took a seat on the board. The board itself would be a good mix of Disrupters, Optimizers, and a few Keepers, ensuring the fiduciary duty was being taken seriously.

The new Optimizer CEO would have likely seen the value of balancing out consultants with a staff. She would have hired a product lead (Optimizer with Disrupter tendencies). Put him in charge of the architecture and data scientist teams. They would partner with one consulting company that could support architecture and data science. Then, they hired a technical lead (Keeper) to ensure everything aligned with the product. Setting the right people from the start would have changed the trajectory of this organization, balancing the need for disruption with the reality of operations.

That lesson is true for any organization, particularly when you're starting something new. Disrupters have value here because they aren't afraid to disrupt. But that only gets you so far. If you try to have Disrupters build stuff, we will, but it won't be sustainable. If you have Keepers at the helm, you'll have a lot of tactical work being done. I call that busy work, but nothing that looks like a plan, strategy, or operational efficiency. Optimizers can bridge the divide. But only if the balance isn't completely off (like a board full of Disrupters or all front-line staff Keepers).

It's Complicated

Then there's the rest of us. The ones who have spent the last twenty years building a data warehouse. A company had jumped on the bandwagon for a data warehouse in the early 2000s. Back then, there weren't many options. You decided between a star schema or data marts and went on your way. The time was spent modeling data into something that reflected how the business worked. Then, you would try to extract it from the source systems, translate it to fit the model, and load it into your shiny new tables. Our use case company did all that. They spent over a decade doing that. Over time, they added consumer layers like PowerBI and tried to do data governance. It was for a long time and, by most accounts, good enough.

Over time, though, the data grew. The models became complex and overlapping. A lot of data and context got lost in the notes of the front-end transactional systems. Data projects became untenable, taking months to complete. The business stakeholders asked a lot of questions about the data. As far as they were concerned, the stuff they saw in their dashboards didn't often reflect what they entered.

The company did what most do. They hired more people. The systems didn't scale anymore, but people do. Sort of. That's where the trouble started. The team that had been there for the last fifteen years didn't appreciate all the new people. They had been a small, tight team that did whatever they needed to complete the job. Most of it wasn't documented, so it wasn't repeatable. They hired a Disrupter to lead the new team. They knew it would require someone with innovative ideas to modernize their systems and ways of doing work. That Disrupter leader did what they all do: started to blow stuff up. He rearranged roles and introduced new tools, technologies, and methods. At first, some people went along because they knew they had to. But it was too much after a while, and the proverbial you-know-what hit you-know-where.

The teams (tenured versus untenured) became more fractured. They refused to work with one another. The untenured team rallied around the leader and followed his standards. The organization was excited about the new capabilities. The untenured team was getting more attention and work. The tenured team became angry and felt unseen and disenfranchised. The culture of the team became untenable. Eventually, the Disrupter leader left. He acknowledged that he probably wasn't the one to bring the team together. You would think that would have been the end, but it wasn't. The tenured team thought that with the leader leaving, they could return to the way it was, but it was too late. The organization got a taste of the new and wanted more.

A Different Outcome

A Disrupter leader needs an Optimizer as a partner. Not right away, and not as a buffer but as someone who takes the disruption and smooths out the edges. People adapt to change differently if they feel like they're part of the process. Optimizers are good at that.

With an Optimizer as the day-to-day manager of the team, the Disrupter could focus on the areas that need that level of attention. The Optimizer could have focused on the team and prepared them for the upcoming changes. Ensuring the manager knew each SDM profile on the team led to a better understanding of their position and why, giving them as many opportunities as possible to feel seen and heard. That's what change management is all about: bringing people along. When organizations take change management seriously, it creates a foundation for expansion, which was the original intention of hiring the Disrupter leader.

Fade to Black

My son is a junior in high school. The end of our parenting journey, at least this phase, is closer every day. I've always kept front and center that preparing him well to leave was my job. His job was to leave. It's hard, of course, because you never feel like you prepare them well enough. That's how I feel here as I consider how to wrap up this book.

AI is a big topic and I hope I did it justice. But for data teams, it is not just about AI—it is about disruption. The sustainable disruption model was built to help people and teams find a way to navigate through changes, big and small. Without question, AI will be a big disruption for data teams. Our ability to reconfigure to meet the demands of the business, reduce technical debt to ensure a strong foundation to build from, and the ability to create a highly functional governance capability will determine success. We all have so much to learn. But building to be future-ready, with the ability to pivot and adjust is the new way forward.

I wish each of you could have been with me along this journey. I started off worried. Now I'm hopeful. That is not to say that there aren't challenges ahead. Or that I wouldn't have made decisions different from those of some of the founders of AI. But I can't rewrite history. What I can do, what you can do, is to take the next step with care. Although we've come to the end of the road, I hope you know I'm out here cheering you on.

Appendix

Book List

O'Neil, Cathy. (2016). Weapons of Math Destruction. Crown Publishing.

Mitchell, Melanie. (2019). Artificial Intelligence: A Guide for Thinking Humans. Picador.

Christian, Brian. (2020). The Alignment Problem: Machine Learning and Human Values. Norton.

Noble, Safiya Umoja. (2018). Algorithms of Oppression: How Search Engines Reinforce Racism. New York University Press.

Bonnell S, and Hansberger A. (2019). Rare Breed: A Guide to Success for the Defiant, Dangerous, and Different. HarperOne.

Benjamin, Ruha. (2022). Viral Justice: How We Grow the World We Want. Princeton.

Russell, Stuart. (2019). Human Compatible: Artificial Intelligence and the Problem of Control. Penguin.

Benjamin, Ruha. (2019). Race After Technology. Polity.

Randolph, Marc. (2019). That Will Never Work. The Birth of Netflix and the Amazing Life of an Idea. Back Bay Books.

Medina, Eden. (2011). Cybernetic Revolutionaries: Technology and Politics in Allende's Chile. MIT Press.

Metz, Cade. (2021). Genius Makers: The Mavericks Who Brought AI to Google, Facebook, and the World. Dutton.

Kurzweil, Ray. (2005). The Singularity is Near: When Humans Transcend Biology. Penguin.

Fletcher, Patti. (2018). Disrupters: Success Strategies from Women who Break the Mold. Entrepreneur Press.

Perez, Carlota. (2002). Technological Revolutions and Financial Capital: The Dynamics of Bubbles and Golden Ages. Edward Elgar Publishing.

Li, Charlene. (2019). The Disruption Mindset: Why Some Organizations Transform While Others Fail. IdeaPress.

Grant, Adam. (2016). Originals: How Non-Conformists Move the World. Penguin.

Johnson, Whitney. (2020). Disrupt Yourself: Master Relentless Change and Speed Up Your Learning Curve. Harvard Business Review Press.

Kotter, J.P., Akhtar, V., and Gupta, G. (2021). Change: How Organizations Achieve Hard-to-Imagine Results in Uncertain and Volatile Times. Wiley.

Iansiti, M. and Lakhani, K.R. (2020). Competing in the Age of AI: Strategy and Leadership When Algorithms and Networks Run the World. Harvard Business Review Press.

Marshall, Brandeis Hill. (2023). Data Conscience: Algorithmic Siege on our Humanity. Wiley.

McGilvray, Danette. (2021). Executing Data Quality Project: Ten Steps to Quality Data and Trusted Information. Academic Press. Second Edition.

Table of Contents for AI Framework Playbook

1) Stated Intention for AI
   a) Mission, Vision Goals
   b) Ethics Overview
   c) Scope
2) Organizational Model
3) RACI
   a) Key Role Descriptions
4) Activities that Support Deployment of AI Technology
   a) Methods for creating a backlog
   b) Building a network of champions
   c) Documenting and ratifying charter
   d) How to document use cases
   e) Identifying Key Stakeholders
   f) Working with Privacy, Compliance, Cybersecurity and Risk Management
   g) Communication Plan
5) Workflows
   a) Change Management
   b) Governance Oversight and Operations
   c) Testing Methodologies (where applicable)
6) Metrics of Success
   a) How to identify metrics
   b) Creating benchmarks
   c) Monitoring metrics

Technical Debt Brief

In this document you include all the details of what you believe to be technical debt. The more information you include the better you can make your case, so take your time.

At a minimum the TDB should include:

- The name or title of the tech debt
- A brief description
- History of how it either became or started as tech debt
  - Why
  - Wh
  - What
  - When
- Your proposed solution
  - Who
  - What
  - When
  - How
  - Duration estimates
  - Cost estimates (work with others as needed)

Index

access governance, 134

ADKAR. See Awareness, Desire, Knowledge, Ability, and Reinforcement

AG. See access governance

AGI. See Artificial General Intelligence

Agile, 122, 158, 176, 180

AI. See artificial intelligence

Alta Vista, 17

Artificial General Intelligence, 16, 19, 22, 37

artificial intelligence, 3, 4, 5, 6, 7, 8, 9, 11, 12, 13, 14, 15, 16, 17, 18, 19, 20, 21, 22, 23, 25, 26, 27, 28, 30, 31, 32, 33, 34, 35, 36, 37, 38, 39, 41, 42, 43, 46, 47, 50, 54, 55, 58, 74, 75, 77, 83, 84, 86, 87, 88, 89, 90, 95, 97, 98, 99, 101, 102, 103, 105, 107, 108, 109, 110, 112, 113, 115, 116, 117, 118, 122, 123, 124, 125, 126, 127, 129, 131, 132, 133, 141, 142, 143, 144, 145, 146, 147, 148, 150, 151, 152, 153, 154, 155, 156, 161, 162, 163, 164, 166, 167, 168, 169, 170, 171, 172, 174, 178, 179, 180, 181, 183, 184, 185, 192

Awareness, Desire, Knowledge, Ability, and Reinforcement, 104

best practices, 6, 146, 152

blockchain, 85

CDO. See Chief Data Officer

ChatGPT, 1, 3, 5, 8, 14, 15, 16, 18, 19, 20, 23, 31, 38, 44, 56, 83, 84, 86, 89, 95, 102, 105, 119, 162, 168, 170

Chief Data Officer, 105, 111, 175

Congress, 147

cybersecurity, 88, 146

DAMA, 32

data catalog, 25, 50, 140

data literacy, 103, 160, 161

Databricks, 46

Dataiku, 46

DataRobot, 46

decentralization, 85

democratization, 106, 144

digital transformation, 85

Disrupters, 54, 55, 62, 64, 66, 70, 72, 74, 75, 89, 90, 91, 92, 93, 94, 95, 97, 98, 132, 174, 187, 188, 194

disruption, 4, 7, 8, 9, 37, 38, 51, 52, 53, 54, 55, 56, 57, 58, 59, 60, 61, 62, 63, 64, 66, 72, 76, 77, 79, 80, 83, 84, 85, 86, 90, 91, 93, 94, 95, 96, 99, 101, 103, 115, 118, 172, 173, 188, 190

DMBOK, 32

electronically stored information, 136

ESI. See electronically stored information

ethics, 12, 27, 28, 148, 150, 151, 152

ETL. See Extract, Transform, Load

existential threat, 6, 11, 112

Extract, Transform, Load, 49, 108

first line of defense, 28, 146

FLOD. See first line of defense

Ford, 29, 33

Formal Methods, 124, 125

Formal Verification, 125

FRAT. See Future-Ready Agile Team

Future-Ready Agile Team, 122

Gartner, 135

General AI, 15

Hofstadter, Douglas, 13

hype, 6, 102, 119, 160, 167, 171, 181

Iger, Bob, 7, 95

Information governance, 135, 136

Internet of Things, 86

IoT. See Internet of Things

Keepers, 54, 55, 62, 66, 70, 72, 74, 75, 78, 81, 90, 94, 97, 98, 110, 117, 122, 131, 142, 143, 145, 162, 173, 174, 175, 179, 188

knowledge graph, 12, 25, 42, 43, 44, 45, 48

Kushner, Dr. Taisa, 126

large language model, 14, 25, 34, 124, 129

LLM. See large language model

machine learning, 2, 3, 5, 8, 12, 15, 16, 18, 26, 30, 34, 36, 48, 84, 87, 123, 126, 127, 129, 144, 163, 164

Marshall, Dr. Brandeis, 148

McGilvray, Danette, 32

Mitchell, Melanie, 37

ML. See machine learning

Moore's Law, 17

Myers Briggs, 60

Narrow AI, 14

natural language processing, 15, 47, 48, 87

Netflix, 94, 99, 193

NLP. See natural language processing

optimistic, 11, 132

Optimizers, 54, 62, 66, 71, 72, 74, 75, 90, 94, 95, 97, 98, 122, 131, 143, 145, 162, 173, 175, 188, 190
Portfolio Management, 136
principles, 40, 41, 47, 149, 181
return on investment, 123, 136
robotic process automation, 87
ROI. See return on investment
sci-fi, 6, 13, 170
SDM, 74, 97, 98, 99, 101, 117, 122, 132, 151, 154, 162, 172, 173, 182, 187, 191, See Sustainable Disruption Model

semantic, 12, 23, 24, 25, 45, 49, 172
structured, 19, 23, 25, 30, 31, 41, 42, 43, 44, 45, 47, 48, 49, 50, 99, 108, 161, 164, 171, 172
supply chain, 44, 88
Sustainable Disruption Model, 54, 62
Tegmark, Max, 125
The Data Governance Institute, 135
time to value, 123
TTV. See time to value
unstructured, 19, 23, 25, 31, 41, 42, 44, 45, 47, 48, 49, 50, 108, 164, 171, 172
virtualization, 49

www.ingramcontent.com/pod-product-compliance
Lightning Source LLC
Chambersburg PA
CBHW071243050326
40690CB00011B/2249